NEVER THE
EASY OPTION

To BANGKOK COL

BEHAVE YOURSELF

NEVER THE EASY OPTION

THE GARETH ELLIS STORY

with Vince Groak

Scratching Shed Publishing Ltd

Typeset in Minion Pro
Printed and bound in the United Kingdom by

Short Run Press Ltd
Bittern Road, Sowton Industrial Estate, Exeter. EX2 7LW
Tel: 01392 211909   Fax: 01392 444134

To my wonderful family – Rachael, Isaac, Eva and Florence.
I love you more than you will ever know.

Contents

My dad wore the Number 10
shirt for Doncaster and Sheffield

Acknowledgements

THERE ARE FAR TOO MANY people to thank for their influence on both myself and my career. So many who have played a huge part in my sporting success, shaping and defining my future.

Old school friends and teachers; teammates and opponents who pushed me to be better every day; every coach I ever had; friends in and away from the sport who have taken me out for a beer or been on the end of the phone when I most needed them; all helped and inspired me to strive to make the best of what I have. I appreciate you all and apologies if I have missed anyone out.

My agent David Howes has guided me perfectly with his advice and hard work behind the scenes. There isn't one difficult decision we made together I regret. I consider you a friend of the family.

For the book, Vince Groak convinced me I had a story to tell and showed patience and commitment to achieving something we can all be proud of. Our meetings and conversations were like therapy sessions post-retirement, which helped no end. Your knowledge of my career and memory of significant moments often surpassed those of my own. I hope you enjoyed our chats as much as I did.

Phil Caplan provided the best biscuits, together with cups of tea, courtesy of Ros. Thank you for all the hard work editing and pulling it all together to create this look at life as a professional sportsman. I am also indebted to stats guru Ian Proctor for my career statistics, and the guys at the Wakefield Trinity Heritage Podcast.

Nothing would have been achieved without my dad, Ken, taxi driver, coach, biggest critic but even greater supporter. Mum Pam and sisters Lynsey, Joanne and Rachel, along with my nephew and nieces Jack, Sam and Gracie, I know you are appreciative of what I have achieved in the sport but one of my greatest achievements is you all being there by my side and sharing the journey together.

It has taken us around the world and allowed us to enjoy some of the greatest days rugby league can offer. There have also been downs, of course, and you have all been the constants of love and support to help get through those times.

My wife and kids have influenced many difficult decisions and made so many sacrifices in support of my career. I hope when the children are old enough to read this you are as proud of me as I am of you and it gives you some understanding of what and who we are.

Rachael, you are an amazing wife and mum. You have always encouraged and supported me, not to mention how you organise us all. Your mum and dad, Stuart and Carol, should be extremely proud of the woman you are.

Appropriately, as I enter the next chapter in my life, I am in no doubt whatsoever that, whatever it entails, none of us will have taken the easy option to get there.

Gareth Ellis
September 2023

Foreword

Dave Trodden

NSWRL CEO and
Former chair of Wests Tigers

I COME FROM A MULTI-GENERATIONAL Balmain family in Sydney. Balmain Tigers (as most people would know) is a foundation club in Australian rugby league, having a proud history extending back to 1908. In 2000, they merged with another foundation club, Western Suburbs, to form Wests Tigers.

For me, love of the Tigers was never a conscious decision, so much as it was a family obligation. I fell into it quite easily and one of the great privileges of my life was to serve as chairman of both Balmain Tigers and Wests Tigers for an extended period of time. By fortunate accident of history, my time as chairman coincided with Gareth Ellis's tenure at the club.

There is no player who has ever played for the Tigers who I have not supported, but there are some who have a special appeal about them. Gareth Ellis was one of those players.

The Tigers, probably more than any other Australian club, have had some amazingly talented English players in their ranks over the years. In 1969, Balmain Tigers scored a historic premiership win against South Sydney, having been guided around the field by the great David Bolton. In 1976, they won they their first midweek cup title on the back of the genius of Brian Lockwood. For one incredible year in 1977, David Topliss was almost untouchable and his five tries in a single match remains a club record.

Garry Schofield made a classy contribution to the club in the early 1980s and, for two months in 1988, Ellery Hanley was arguably the best player in the world during a run which took the Tigers all the way to the grand final. A year later, Andy Currier's goalkicking almost secured an elusive premiership victory.

Great though all of those players were – and wonderful though their individual contributions all were – none of them had the sustained impact on the club that Gareth did over four breathtaking years from 2009 to 2012.

Gareth personified professionalism and had the quiet strength and controlled aggression about his play that all of his teammates fed off and were inspired by. It wasn't all about toughness though. There was a memorable moment in Auckland against the Warriors when a try was created from a reverse flick pass of a quality Benji Marshall would have been proud of.

It does Gareth a disservice to reduce his Tigers career to statistics, but one is worth mentioning. He was player of the year for Wests Tigers in three of the four years he played with them (2009, 2010 and 2011). To put that into context, in those years talents such as Benji, Robbie Farah, Lote Tuqiri, Chris Lawrence, Keith Galloway and Todd Payten played with the club. For Gareth to be consistently pre-eminent in that outstanding group says it all. The fact no other player in the history of Wests Tigers has won the award three times (much less three times in succession), probably puts the exclamation mark to the statement, but that would be unnecessary. During those years, there was no better player in his position in the NRL than Gareth Ellis.

One of the opportunities that sport provides is the ability to forge enduring friendships. Gareth, to Elaine and our family, was much more than a great footballer. To us, Gareth and his family were part of our family. Even now, Gareth's sister Rachel meets up with our daughter Samantha in various corners of the world when their schedules allow, and there is never a weekend in the football season when text messages are not exchanged with Gareth's dad, Ken, solving the problems of the rugby league world and keeping up to date with the lives of him and Pam. Our son, Matthew, constantly reminds us that Gareth's son, Isaac, qualifies to play for Australia having been born here. Make sure you remember that Gareth when the time comes along!

Gareth was much loved by all of the Wests Tigers fans. When the Premier of New South Wales, the Hon. Barry O'Farrell (a Tigers fan), turned up at a birthday party for Gareth's nephew Jack, he was actually paying homage on behalf of our whole state to one of the most respected footballers playing in the NRL at the time. Such is the respect that Gareth enjoyed.

It is a great privilege for me to contribute to his story. Gareth Ellis, champion footballer, even better bloke.

David Trodden
September 2023

NEVER THE
EASY OPTION

1

Breaking the Hoodoo

27 August 2016
Wembley Stadium

THE HOOTER HAS GONE and so have I. I'm absolutely shattered, drained and all I can do is put my hands on my knees and take great big gulps of Wembley air. Before I know it, everyone is jumping on me, leaping on each other, and just cavorting around.

We did it. We really did it.

Legendary player David Topliss had told me much earlier in my career, and with seeming prescience: 'Win the Challenge Cup at Wembley with Hull FC and you'll go down in folklore.' Toppo's words aren't far from my mind as I start the walk up the Wembley steps. I'd won trophies before, Grand Finals, World Club Challenges, but the Challenge Cup had eluded me and I'd never won anything as a captain. This was going to be the first time I would lift a major trophy and I was determined to remember every second of it.

I take my steps slowly and try to take pictures in my mind of everything I see and do. Hands reach out to grab mine, slap my back, shout their congratulations. Somewhere, halfway up the steps, someone gives me a black and white scarf and I tie it around my neck and then I realise that almost every Hull supporter I see is crying. Tears of joy everywhere I look, that's when it really hit home.

Later, people will never stop telling me what this day meant to them after years of supporting the club. Or they'd detail me about their dad, or grandmother, who had died before they had the chance to see Hull win at Wembley. But, instead of sadness, there is elation. We hadn't just done it for the multitude that were there, it was for the hundreds of thousands, over the decades, who had dreamed of this day. We knew exactly what it meant to the supporters who had been tortured by a song about never winning at Wembley – not least by their bitter rivals in the east of the city – which was now consigned to history; that's why it was so emotional for all of us.

I pause briefly at the top of the stairs and try to compose myself. I take the scarf off and stick it in my shorts. For some reason I don't want it getting in the way of my medal, and then we are on the balcony and I walk past Kevin Sinfield and the dignitaries including beaming Hull chairman Adam Pearson, who all speak to me, but I'm not really listening. I pause and shake hands with Lizzie Jones, who is presenting the glorious trophy, and get myself ready. All the lads are to my left as she hands me the cherished silverware.

At that moment, I remember going to watch my boyhood team, Castleford, at Wembley a few times, starting in 1986 when they beat Hull KR. Seeing and getting to appreciate all the traditions of the Cup ... suit with carnation beforehand ... civic receptions ... it was as if I'd gone back in time to being that kid. To think that the youngster who'd watched in awe was doing it himself now was surreal.

Lifting the Challenge Cup at Wembley was the best feeling I ever experienced in rugby league; kissing the gorgeous trophy, holding it up for the Hull fans and hearing their roar, absolutely unbelievable and almost indescribable. Now, I worry that nothing I will ever do again in life will make me feel so joyous or move me in such a way.

That 2016 triumph wasn't just about winning at Wembley, for me it was also about that decision I made in 2012 to sign for Hull, and it was about breaking my foot at Leeds, of all places, before my debut for them. It was about sacrificing my international career to focus on playing in those famed black and white irregular hoops. But then it was about a torn Achilles and the doubts over whether I would play again, and of all the times I feared my career would fizzle out.

At the time, I had a year left on my contract and decided to give it another crack and knuckle down. As anyone who's been injured playing sport will know, you're quite isolated and distanced from the team. It becomes very much a mental battle, sees what you're about. Can you work hard when no-one is watching you? That was the challenge for me, and I embraced it, got stuck into it and in 2016, at the age of 36, had one of the best years of my career.

A week before the final, I was driving home from the Man of Steel awards ceremony. Danny Houghton sat next to me, Lee Radford in the back. Lee had won Coach of the Year and Danny narrowly pipped me to become the Steve Prescott Man of Steel, but his best was yet to come with the tackle that won us the Cup.

Ben Currie seemed a certain scorer for Warrington, they were going to take away the biggest prize from us in the last minute, but the so-called 'Tackle 52' – as it was the fifty-second Danny had made in the game – saved the day. One tackle which changed the history of Hull FC and helped redefine how I think about my career.

One month after Wembley, I went to a function at Beverley Racecourse with the trophy there, pride of place on a plinth in the middle of the main enclosure. By then it had just come back from the engravers. I knew the plaques around the bottom recalled all the winning teams going back to 1897 but hadn't realised the captains' names were also recorded. Seeing 'Hull FC, 2016, G. Ellis' for the first time, tears were back in my eyes. I love the thought of legacy, what you've done to leave an impact. I was told the Challenge Cup is the only major sports trophy that has the name of the skipper of the winning side engraved on it. I got out my phone and took a picture. 'That will always be there,' I thought, and another speck of dust blew into my eye! No one can take that away. It still fills me with so much pride that I was fortunate enough to lead that team out.

In 2022, I was inducted into the Hull FC Hall of Fame on the back of those Cup exploits and it was equally special. You go through your career trying to be the best player you can and sometimes you doubt yourself, I always have, so to be recognised as having some influence and be among those considered the greatest to have worn the iconic shirt is very humbling and something else I'm proud of.

When you start out as a kid playing the game, you never think about such accolades and recognition, but as you get older you do reflect a little bit more on your career, so inductions like that are very special. Playing is the ultimate – the moments you share with your teammates both in training and matches – and the pinnacle of that is lifting silverware, but when it has a wider impact it's terrific.

Unbeknown to me beforehand, my family were in attendance at the Hall of Fame dinner to see it, which made it extra special. They play a huge part in who I am as a person and player; they're the ones who pick you back up and put a smile on your face when all you might want to do is lock yourself in a room, particularly after some of the tough injuries I've had.

There were some great montages and tributes from ex-players as I went up to accept the award. Those kinds of compliments and acceptance when you are part of a team game is incredibly humbling especially as, throughout my career, I always felt a measure of imposter syndrome.

This is a book that deals in fine margins and close calls. It's a story of big decisions, tough choices and lucky breaks. But, more than anything, it's about hard work. Danny Houghton didn't make that tackle at Wembley because he was lucky. He did it because he is the fittest man I have ever played with and because he goes full-on for eighty minutes. And I didn't get to lift the Challenge Cup at the age I was because I got lucky, it was because I took a risk, made sacrifices and kept going despite setbacks.

I often contemplate the life I could have lived.

Mine, like everyone's I suppose, has been filled with pivotal moments. If I had got an apprenticeship at Church Fenton ... if my dad had taken me home instead of coaxing me out of the car at my first Wakefield training session ... if Tom Haughey hadn't gone part-time at Trinity and given me the opportunity as an apprentice instead ... if I hadn't been coached by John Harbin ... if I'd signed for Bradford instead of Leeds, Leeds instead of Wests Tigers, or Leeds again instead of Hull.

If Danny Houghton hadn't made that tackle at Wembley would my mistimed one on Joe Westerman just before it have cost us the

Cup? How differently would I reflect on my time at Hull if we hadn't won it first time and would we have retained it? Probably not.

I still wonder how I came to retire in 2017, but then came back a year-and-a-half later. Until that point, my career had a certain narrative and order to it, then it all becomes quite messy. But even then, I look back on that difficult time as a period in which I learned a lot about myself, mostly things I couldn't do very well. It was similar to being an apprentice again at Wakefield, but necessary.

I was incredibly grateful to play again. I did retire too soon, no doubt. From the start of the 2017 season, in the mud at Belle Vue, I was mentally shattered. I underestimated what the preceding half-decade had taken out of me. The lows of 2013 and 2015 were all vindicated at Wembley the following year. After that outpouring of joy and relief, I had little left to give.

I felt lost yet found a different way to contribute, but then this is also a story of never taking the easy option.

2

Decisions

WHEN I DECIDED TO come back from playing in Australia after four years, my first thoughts were to return to Leeds. They were in the midst of their golden generation run of success, which I'd already been a part of; they were interested – hang your kit on the peg you left – so the obvious solution. What I also knew from my experiences to that point was that whenever I had stepped out of my comfort zone, however reluctantly, it brought the best out of me.

I'd been a young lad playing for Castleford Lock Lane U18s. I had a year in the York academy ranks, but most of my contemporaries who were any good had been picked up and signed, already making their way in the game. Then, towards the back end of 1998, I got picked to play for the Yorkshire age group side. Wakefield had just been promoted to Super League for the first time and a requirement was that they had to have an academy side to mirror the senior team's fixtures, so they looked to pull one together.

I had a freakishly good game that day and, luckily, Trinity head coach John Harbin, in his Canberra Raiders tracksuit top, which his son Lionel must have given him, and assistant Andy Kelly witnessed it. They spoke to my dad afterwards but I didn't think anything of it.

He told me they'd asked if I might want to train at Featherstone High School with them. Dad took me to the first one and I was scared stiff I'd be mixing with a group of the best kids they'd scouted. I refused to get out of the car, told dad I didn't want to do it such was my self-doubt. A few choice words later, he implored me to at least give it a go. Sulky teenagers, your parents *are* right sometimes.

I absolutely loved it. I was made to feel extremely welcome by guys like Tiger Handforth, Ben Westwood and Tom Haughey, and I'm forever grateful for that opportunity which lasted six memorable years. Wakefield is a club I still hold dear for that reason.

I hadn't been good enough to be picked up by a professional club at the age most kids identified with talent are. Up until my mid-teens I was quite small. It was only at 15, when I had a growth spurt, that I began to feel more confident to mix it with those becoming men. I'm grateful it turned out that way because I don't think I would have got the opportunities I eventually did as a later developer. Better players than me, snapped up earlier and going to Castleford and then a number to Bradford or Leeds, had their progress blocked by more established guys and couldn't break through.

The reserve league was fundamental to my development; facing established, experienced professionals, together with young guns like me who were desperate to prove themselves in my position, it was a constant challenge. I learned many valuable lessons for when my chance came. The competitive nature I had in me was stoked.

My debut for Trinity came in September 1999 against Wigan, only months after I'd joined as an apprentice, going from playing in Academy curtain-raisers before Super League games to being in one. Tom was on the scheme but travelling over from Keighley, which was costing him more than he was being paid and he asked to go part-time, which the club agreed to. That opened up a space for an apprentice and I'd just finished college – again it was a case of right place, right time. Steve Ferres, CEO back then, asked if I'd like to take the spot over and, as I had no firm plans of what I wanted to do, I thought 'why not?'.

Eventually leaving Wakefield wasn't straightforward. My career was starting to kick on and I began thinking about winning things and how I could establish myself as a Great Britain international. I was still very happy at Trinity, 2004 had been a turning point season, but I had to determine where I was going.

I'd been shown a model of how Belle Vue would look when I originally signed – and three or four others since – but were they really the ambitions of the club, or was it going to return to the mindset of just surviving? I used to speak to David Topliss a lot around that time, and he advised me that he felt that he might have stayed at the club a little too long and missed out on claiming some of the big trophies and glory years as a result. He never once told me to leave Belle Vue, where he was loved, but that resonated with me, I needed to make a calculated decision about the unknown. I had consciously to think about what I wanted to achieve in the sport, rather than make the best of what I had. To stay with the easy option, especially with a year left on my existing deal.

I was also aware that Trinity would be happy if they could make some money from a transfer fee. At one stage it looked far more likely I'd be going to Bradford, if anywhere. I didn't get involved in any of the negotiations behind the scenes, I was just happy to keep concentrating on what I could do best.

Wakefield coach Shane McNally asked me what was happening because he'd been given the phone numbers of a couple of Bulls players who were supposedly part of a swap deal, but when he called them they knew nothing about it. I didn't want to have anything to do with that and decided to stay at Trinity and see how things went for another year, which I was quite happy about.

Christmas came along and Wakefield wanted me to sign another deal, but this time I was reluctant to commit. When we played against Leeds on Boxing Day in the traditional friendly fixture and got hammered I started to question where Trinity were going. The Rhinos had been interested initially, however their offer wasn't as high as Bradford's. Eventually they came back with terms Wakefield were happy with and, in the end, the transfer agreement happened really fast. It felt right to kick on. It was hard because I owed so much to Wakefield for the opportunity they'd given me; they'd been the only ones prepared to take a chance on me after all.

There was a similar feeling of trepidation of the unknown when I left Leeds after winning a second Grand Final in 2008, to join Wests Tigers in the NRL. A few Wakefield players like Matt Seers, Nathan Wood and particularly Troy Slattery, hinted over the years that I should give it a crack in the elite Australian competition. I didn't really think much of it at the time, but they were the first ones to give me a nudge in that direction.

In 2006, I played with Mark O'Neill at Leeds, who had come from Wests Tigers and won a Grand Final there; he was the one now who kept pushing me. Leeds didn't have a great season that year, but I went well and Mark was constantly on to their head coach Tim Sheens telling him about me and instigated the move.

Again, though, I was torn. I was part of a team that was winning at the top level and could tell that success was going to continue. But, at 27, I knew that I was either going to sign another contract to stay at Headingley for four more years and finish my career there, or I was again going to bite the bullet, step outside my comfort zone, and pack my bags for Australia.

I talked with Leeds CEO Gary Hetherington a few times, too-ed and fro-ed in my own mind, until I decided I was going to stay in Yorkshire. But then, in one of those final meetings, which included both my dad and agent David Howes, I got a sense of Gary having an air of me not being able to make a go of it down under.

Although I don't think he meant it, I could feel myself bristling and thought 'I'll show you'. As we left the meeting I told the others I was definitely going. Looking back, I don't regret it one bit, even though I didn't win any silverware at Wests Tigers. A lot of it is to do with the life experience and for me it felt almost like being on a working holiday all the time I was over there. I had a job to do, one that I was exceptionally keen to leave my mark on, but it was an adventure.

How the Tigers looked after me, and welcomed us, was first class. They also had one of the most spirited dressing rooms I have ever been part of.

3

Culture

IT'S MONDAY MORNING, a few days after we lost on Friday. We didn't just lose though, we were beaten in every aspect of the game. I can cope with defeat, but I can't just ignore it. I have been looking forward to training this morning, time to put it right and start preparing for the next game. I'm up early, coffee, smoothie, and then I jump in the car. I pull into the training ground just before eight and I'm into my kit quickly. The session is about to start and we're all ready to go.

Then I hear a car pull into the car park, tyres screeching on gravel. One of my teammates is cutting it fine. Laughing and joking as he waltzes into the changing room with his bag swung over his shoulder, I feel my jaw clench. He sits down opposite me and starts getting his stuff together, no rush. It's only been two and a half days since we were played off the park. The man opposite me had missed tackles, made errors and here he is, not a care in the world. I want to say something, but I don't know where to start or how it will end. I don't want a fight or confrontation, I just want him to give a shit.

I want him to want to play better next week and understand that what he does this morning, tomorrow and the next day has an impact on what he does next Friday. I reach down, tie my laces deliberately, firmly. I stamp my feet, make a big deal of checking my kit and then walk past him, with purpose. As I do, he stands up and I catch the smell on his breath. He stinks of ale. I curl my fist, I'm fuming. I went to bed at ten the previous night to get enough sleep to train the house down today while he was... Well, God knows where he was, or what he was doing. I want to have a go at him. I'm his captain, I'm entitled to bawl him out, but I don't, I can't. I walk past him, out of the dressing room and onto the training ground. I work my arse off, train like I'm on some kind of trial. I hope that he is watching me and is shamed in some way.

When I became captain at Hull, it gave me license to speak out; it probably became my duty. But, in the early days, when attitudes were not what they needed to be, I didn't say anything. That's not to say I was indifferent to under-performance, far from it. Some of the lads told me that my body language and the way I looked at someone was enough to express my displeasure. I spoke in team meetings and I had no problem taking a younger player aside, offering advice, knowing they might listen and learn.

I spent all my career wanting to be a player others wanted to play alongside – that's what motivated me, the respect of my teammates. To be able to do that is partly dependent on the 'culture' surrounding a group, a nebulous often spoken of concept hard to define.

I wasn't the same person on the field as I was off it. If I had been, I wouldn't have made it. You come across some who can't make that differentiation. I'm told my dad was a bit feisty when he put the boots on and earned a few yellow and red cards in his time, and maybe that's where it comes from, but I just had this overwhelming desire to compete.

A lot of it comes from wanting to prove that I was worthy to play alongside my peers. I was there for them, to back them up, that's what fired me up the most. I used to get really annoyed when I heard players talking about others in my position and remember thinking, 'I'll show them who's the best'. It was that instinct and attitude that was the difference for me.

I made everything into a personal battle and was determined

never to show any form of weakness, to ensure that I physically and mentally tried to break my opponents. For me, the game should be played right on the edge and, inevitably, it's a fine line. On occasions you are going to cross it and either give away a penalty or spend a period in the sin-bin, that's an occupational hazard.

When I began playing, every game was like my life depended on it. I would spend most of the day of it ruminating about what I needed to do. I'd over-think it. By the time the match came around I had played it over in my head so many times that I was almost exhausted before I even got onto the field.

I didn't ever shed that feeling of trying to fit in by working hard to be accepted, that was really important for me. I was the complete opposite to someone like Michael Jordan, in basketball, who just had supreme confidence and belief from an early age. A lot of being nervous before every single game, even at the age of 39, was down to that. On game day, negative thoughts used to come into my head about missing a crucial tackle or dropping the ball with the line open and letting my teammates down. It was only over time that I learned to manage that. What I did know was that I'd done the work to be able to correct it. That came from people like John Harbin installing that effort-based mentality into me.

When I first broke through at Wakefield, off-the-field problems brought the players closer together. Trinity's culture was exactly what was required by that group. They needed to enjoy each other's company and togetherness, that was their strength. It was us against them. If we couldn't rely on the directors, we bonded together to look after each other and there were some great blokes in the mix.

Gary Price was one of those old-school types who carried himself with an air of authority, which held the younger players in awe. But he was the friendliest and most approachable of senior professionals with a great sense of humour. Willie Poching and Andy Fisher were much the same.

The March brothers were a bit older than me but establishing themselves in the first team while I was an apprentice. I became good friends with David and his wife Corina, who looked out for me in many different ways, giving me lifts to training or letting me crash at their house after a night out at The Frontier in Batley. We would never have been considered a partying team, but we enjoyed a social, sometimes after training and usually after a game. That though was always, especially for the younger lads, on a Monday, which just happened to be 'student night' in Wakefield. If we went out, then Tuesday mornings became a challenge, but it was one that I relished. I never missed a session. There was an expectation that anyone who had been out clubbing would be the first to training the next day and would push themselves to be at the front of everything.

The speed of my rise meant that if I was going to be successful, I had to be the best version of myself otherwise I would have been picked up earlier on talent alone, and I was acutely aware of that. It worked out to be a blessing. You see loads of gifted players around but they overly rely on knowing that they have natural ability. In order to get to the next level, they don't appreciate how to work hard to achieve that and get lost in the system. Talent can only get you so far before you fall by the wayside. I was the opposite.

Going to Leeds was what I expected. The jailing of young stars Chev Walker and Ryan Bailey, following a drunken brawl in the city centre in 2003, probably defined a lot of the culture there at that time. Ryan was a loveable rouge, despised by many opponents on the field, but such a hard worker in training whose effort I really admired. That incident instigated a change of direction in deciding what the club wanted to be and be known as – a brand the city could be proud of. Putting rules in place, such as the need to ring head coach Tony Smith before you went on a night out, emanated from that. It was like having another parent or a teacher. He never said no, but his theory was that if you knew that he knew you were out, you would then behave appropriately.

Some players didn't like it, but having it there made you think about your actions. That's what Tony was good at, playing those mind games and it had the desired effect. He got the buy-in – particularly from the core group – as to what it took to win and it began to work on the field. Influencing it were some very good people too.

At Headingley, it took years to build a winning culture after decades of under achievement and they were also fortunate to discover a group of special players that came through the youth team at the same time. The culture at Leeds is based around being the absolute best in everything you do. They also had Tony at the heart of it, someone with clear standards from which he never wavered.

As a Castleford supporter growing up, we always took great pleasure in watching Leeds struggle, but when I joined the Rhinos, things were different. The club had invested in its youth, played the long game and it was about to pay off. Tony's attention to detail and idiosyncratic quirks meant that he needed time to convince the players that his approach of relentless perseverance would work. By 2007, everyone was totally invested in the culture.

We had some great days out together, go-karting, paintballing and the like. It was great fun. Those hours we spent together brought us closer on a personal level and made a difference. We were also expected to do our bit for the sponsors and wider community. Each week we were given a printed schedule that set out our itinerary and listed the events at which we had to represent the club. We didn't give much thought to what we were asked to do, we just did as we were told. One day, I looked at mine to find that I was due to judge a 'Best in Show' dog competition in Harrogate. My wife Rachael and I had recently bought a dog, loved it and I probably went on about it a bit at training. Kylie Leuluai was also scheduled to go with me; we thought it a bit odd but didn't say much about it.

One or two other lads seemed unusually interested in where they had been allocated to go as well and I began to suspect something was amiss. But it was only when Rob Burrow came into the team room shouting: 'What am I doing at a dwarf throwing competition?' that we realised we were having our legs pulled. Jamie Peacock was rolling around on the floor, tears streaming down his face. There's nothing like a good wind-up for team spirit, that's for sure.

Culture is not easy to put into practice, especially when the pressure is on or thousands of fans are calling for your head. That's when you feel the temptation to break from the plan and go out and sign a marquee player who might win you some big games. But if he doesn't bring the right ethos to the group, young impressionable players are going to learn the wrong way to conduct themselves and that is going to cause you many more problems down the line.

There are always times with every club where you go through a period which tests the road you have mapped out. But, if you truly believe in the standards and behaviours you have created, then is not the time to jump ship. At Hull, we lost seven games in a row at the start of the 2023 season, but Tony Smith and Adam Pearson stayed firm and the results of that will be seen in the longer term.

The fans are astute. They value effort and won't accept anything less. But in the past Hull has often fallen into the trap of over-promising and under-delivering. When we tell them, 'We've got a squad that can win something this year,' they probably roll their eyes. What they should discuss is that they're holding everyone to account to the highest standards and that they won't sign or re-sign anyone who can't meet those expectations. They can't promise they will win anything, but will be striving to be a better team and club than the previous year, and the following one will be better again. The fans know their team can beat anyone on their day, but they've also seen them get hammered far too many times in the past few years and know that a bunch of fragile players rarely go on to win anything.

Those kinds of messages matter. If you want your supporters to stick with you, and be patient, you have to explain to them what you are about and what you are aiming to achieve in the short, medium and long term.

I feel equipped to talk about culture because I have seen so many different versions and what works and what doesn't. The one at Wests Tigers was quite freewheeling, although the team spirit among the players was as good as I ever experienced. But the responsibility for that was with them. Although the club planned, and encouraged, a lot of the social activities, it was the players who were responsible for the 'brothers forever' culture and, once the core began to move on in 2012, the Tigers quickly slipped and lost their way.

I've always been impressed by Wigan's DNA. It is so deeply embedded that it must be hard to locate the source of it. They have the advantage of an enviable youth structure and are financially solid, but it runs deeper than that. All the youngsters who come through the ranks are moulded into exactly the type of players and people the club wants them to be. That comes from having absolute clarity on standards and how they expect things to be done. Their coaching systems and back-office teams are really stable so that the personnel evolve and there are no breaks in continuity. You never hear anyone at Wigan saying: 'It's time for a clear out.' They tend to appoint coaches from within who share the values and it works.

But it was at Melbourne that I probably learned the most about what culture means. Frank Ponissi has been the football manager at Storm for more than a decade and, together with head coach Craig Bellamy, they have developed arguably the best footballing department in world rugby. Aware that my playing days were coming to an end, David Howes fixed up a visit for me and, in the middle of the 2018 season, I flew out there.

Typically, Ponissi doesn't waste anyone's time and I was presented with a very busy schedule when I arrived. I had complete access to every aspect of their operation and one of my first meetings was with Frank himself. 'There's no magic secret,' he told me. 'No silver bullet to explain what we do here. We just work hard and try to get all of the little bits right all the time. If you turned up to our training session on a Monday morning,' he went on, 'you wouldn't be able to tell whether we'd won or lost. The accountability for performance is exactly the same.' I watched them analyse two games while I was there (a win and a defeat) and there was no difference. They just focused on the process, never the outcome.

Under Bellamy, the players were held to account for everything they did. It was all about the mental approach and ensuring that levels of concentration and effort never dropped. At the time of my visit, my ambitions were turning towards coaching and, as I listened to him during that week, a light was going on in my head. This was a side to coaching that I had not seen much of, certainly not to the same degree. The focus on standards, behaviours and accountability was totally aligned with my own views on the game.

I was also impressed by the man-management methods. Craig and his wife hosted a dinner at their home for all the wives and girlfriends to thank them for their support over the course of the season. He also took time out to have a coffee with Cameron Munster, a young player with a very bright future ahead of him. When I asked why they were meeting up, Craig just told me, 'No reason. There doesn't need to be a reason for me to sit and chat to one of our players, check in on him to see how he's going.' Munster signed a five-year contract with the Storm shortly afterwards and is now one of the sport's very best.

Melbourne, one of the most consistently successful clubs in the toughest competition, have a very strong culture of improvement. If you are training to maintain, then you are training to fail – that is their mantra. Players spoke of brutal sessions and expletive-heavy rollockings, but yet they had the utmost respect for their coach; they knew exactly where they stood. He would rip into them because he wanted them to get better, but then treat them with such affection and care on a personal level.

Another aspect of a winning culture is having a thirst for new ideas and the humility to accept that you do not have all the answers. That's something else Melbourne do well. Most years, Craig and Frank will visit other sports clubs around the world in search of new methods and inspiration.

Occasionally, we brought in some guest speakers to Hull and I was always very open-minded to hear what they had to say. I figure that if I only pick up one message or learn a single new aspect, then it will have been worth my time and that hasn't stopped me trying to learn some new techniques myself. I'm not a huge reader, but I tend to opt for books on motivation. I'm a big believer in learning whatever I can from people that have been successful in other fields.

You can also see the Melbourne culture in the way they attract new players in what is still a development area for the sport. They have a team of recruitment officers who scour the youth leagues, junior competitions, country leagues, analysing the statistics and spotting the talent. But they don't contract anyone until Bellamy has run the rule over them. 'I don't sign anyone,' he told me, 'without meeting them face to face, at least twice. I want to know what kind of a bloke I am getting before they sign for the Storm.'

To illustrate that point, he went on to tell me about a junior player they had lined up to bring in a few years earlier. He was one of the hottest properties in the game but when he met Bellamy he did not impress. He spent most of his time checking his phone for messages and even put his feet up on a chair next to him. Needless to say, Bellyache passed and the lad signed for another club on a record contract. Twelve months later, he had moved on again and the kid still hasn't fulfilled his promise.

I have never come across an English club that has the same ruthlessly forensic approach to recruitment. Frank was quick to acknowledge that, over the past fifteen years, they had arguably been served by three of the best players ever to play the game in Cameron Smith, Cooper Cronk and Billy Slater. But the crucial point is that not only were they world-class performers, but also the club's hardest working players, setting the standard for everyone else there. If you don't work to achieve those standards, you won't last long at Melbourne. It is such a strong, positive environment and that just isn't up for negotiation.

I've never had what it takes to be a coach. I have never possessed what I would describe as the technical know-how to analyse a game, never mind the ability to conjure up a tactical plan to win one. Yet what I saw in Melbourne was a philosophy I did understand. You work hard, are honest with yourself and teammates and strive for continual improvement, no matter how small.

Culture is hard to define, I don't think there are set or specific guidelines for it. It has been different at every club I've been at, but if there is a common factor, it is that the players really cared – about the team, each other and winning. Each and every decision was made with those goals in mind. Now in retirement, I reckon I probably sacrificed some relationships in my quest. I very rarely see the people I went to school with because once I committed to rugby, I couldn't socialise with them. But would I change anything?

No, because that's the path I chose.

4

Influences

THERE ARE TIMES IN everyone's life when someone steps from the shadows and changes yours. For me, that happened when I first met John Harbin.

In 1998, I was still a skinny seventeen-year-old turning out for Lock Lane U18s. I'd played a few times for their reserves and was expected, in time, to progress to the first team and that would be that. Nobody ever said anything about playing professionally. But then I had that growth spurt and, within months, was one of the tallest lads in the side.

After a spell playing for York Academy that summer, I went back to Lock Lane, suddenly one of their best. I was big, powerful and capable of dominating games. My performances at the start of the following season caught the attention of Wakefield scout John Holroyd and led to the call-up for Yorkshire U18s, against Lancashire, when unbeknownst to me Trinity coach Andy Kelly and John Harbin, their development officer, were also in the crowd and asked my dad if I'd be interested in training with their academy. As delighted as I was, I could feel anxiety building and the closer we got to Featherstone High School, the venue, the quieter I got, totally lacking in self-belief. The other lads seemed confident, more at ease and I didn't feel that I belonged. Somehow, though, once dad got me out of the car, I began to feel more comfortable with John in charge. I listened to everything he said, keen to hear more. I didn't speak to anyone unless I had to, but tried as hard as I could in everything he asked me to do. The only way I could make my mark was to earn respect by doing everything as well as they did. The fish and chips on the way home, which became something of a ritual, tasted good.

John Harbin is a Yorkshireman by birth but had spent most of his life in Australia after emigrating with his parents as a child. After working as a teacher, he returned to Yorkshire and joined Wakefield as youth coach. I've been fortunate to work for some great coaches. More than anything, I have been lucky to come across the right one at the right time and working under John at that period had a huge impact. He used to say that no matter what you're doing, aim to be the best. 'If you're in the gym, try to lift as much as you possibly can. Even if you're just having a team run around the pitch, always make sure you're out front.' His words stuck with me and resonate still.

By any standards, the group that made up Wakefield's academy team in 1999 were a rare breed. There were around twenty of us and a few – Tom Haughey, Paul 'Tiger' Handforth and Ben Westwood – were already on apprentice terms. There were some real characters but John was undoubtedly our leader. He had an air of authority and yet was a father figure. One day, when the first team were struggling to get results, he put a sign on the training ground in front of the area on which the academy team was training. 'Men at Work' it read. He must have picked it up from some roadworks. It made us feel ten foot tall and probably pissed the senior players off a bit. John didn't mind. Everything he did was calculated to get a reaction and did.

Our fixtures began in March and although we lost our first twelve games John never wavered in his determination that we should continue doing our thing, preparing and playing our way. We played a few curtain-raisers before first team games and I recall going to Odsal and the Boulevard. Each game, no matter the result, was a learning experience for us all and John never missed a chance to build us up, to talk to us about the great futures we had ahead of us.

In mid-season, we played an open trial game against the juniors (what would be the scholarship team nowadays) and, although we beat them, it was a really competitive match which resulted in seven of them joining up with the Academy squad, including Chris Feather, who was a friend of Tom's from Keighley, and a cheeky little half-back called Danny Brough. From that moment on, we won ten of our last twelve games almost making it to the play-offs.

'One more round,' John would always say, which became our motto. If we were camped on our line defending, someone would shout it and you could see everyone dig that little bit deeper. At first, I hoped that John would see me going into the gym for 'extras' but, after a while, I wasn't bothered whether anyone saw me or not. I had begun to realise that it was the right thing to do.

John wanted us to aim high. One day, he sat the apprentices down after training and asked us, in turn, about our ambitions in the game. One by one, we all talked about wanting to be a first-teamer, having a career at Wakefield and so on. When it came to my turn, I just copied what everyone else had said. After a while, frustrated, he stopped and asked us: 'Why do none of you want to play for Great Britain? Why set your sights so low? Always aim for the top,' he said.

I've always trained really hard and when we were apprentices at Wakefield, we'd be at the ground from nine until five, like in a proper job. When we weren't training we'd be cleaning boots, sweeping the grounds and in the off-season painting the changing rooms – and getting shouted at by Steve 'the bath', the groundsman and kit man who was nominally in charge of us.

Danny used to really annoy him, especially when we'd pick a target – a floodlight or the closed-up burger van – and play kick golf. One day John called me in just as we were leaving and said: 'Do you think that's the best use of your time? Is kicking a ball around going to make the difference for someone like you?'

I remember going away and thinking he was right. It was perfect for Broughy, but wouldn't add anything to my game. He told me to go and get another gym or weights programme and, from then on, when I had any spare time took in an extra session. Comments like that made me realise that I needed to work even harder and wasn't good enough. I put a lot of trust in all the coaches I had, knowing that what they were telling me was for my benefit. I rarely questioned things and in return gave them my all. In the early days at Wakefield, we went through several different coaches, which was unsettling because people I'd put a lot of trust in and who'd had faith in me moved on pretty quickly.

As much as I was enjoying playing for Wakefield's academy, I had now turned eighteen and was about to leave college. Thoughts of what lay ahead arose and I began to apply for jobs. Aware of this, John asked my dad: 'Would he be interested in becoming an apprentice at Wakefield?' Well, I was never going to knock back that kind of opportunity. Presented with a contract, I signed on the dotted line and, on 15 July 1999 became a professional rugby league player, on six grand a year. Apprentice terms didn't mean I was guaranteed a career. The job was far from glamorous and I faced huge hurdles before I could even think of making it.

For one thing, it took me ages to get to the ground. Most days, dad and I would leave Selby early so he could drop me off at Castleford bus station before he went to work. From there, it was two buses to Wakefield. Afterwards, I'd get the bus back to Castleford and walk to my Auntie Jean's house, where I would wait until my dad came to pick me up after he finished work. It meant long days for the pair of us and, if dad was working away, I would have to get the bus from Selby, which was like a magical mystery tour and would take nearly two and a half hours to reach Wakefield.

By then, there were five full-time apprentices – 'Tiger' Handforth, Ben Westwood, Danny Brough, Keith Mason and me. Our first job when we arrived on a Monday morning was to help Steve clean the ground after the previous day's game. Loaded up with black bin bags, we set about sweeping the rubbish into piles before joining him indoors to clean the first-team players' boots and sweep the dressing rooms. With our chores complete, we could then join the first team players in weights and field sessions, which made it all worthwhile. On Tuesdays and Thursdays, we would hang around the ground waiting for the part-time players to arrive for academy training in the evening. It was a demanding routine but we all loved it.

On the back of the success we had as an academy team, a few of the lads were called up to play in Wakefield's 'A' team towards the end of the season. I found it a big step-up to be playing against fully-grown men, some in their thirties, but it was a challenge to which I quickly adjusted. After a taste I was keen for more, but Andy Kelly had an even bigger prize in mind.

It had been a tough first season in Super League for Trinity, but with no threat of relegation Andy decided to give an opportunity to some of his younger players in the final games of the campaign. On the penultimate weekend, Ben Westwood got his chance, selected on the bench for the trip to Gateshead. But then, the week after, he was horsing around at home climbing on top of a shed to throw off one of those plastic toy soldiers with a parachute on its back, slipped through the roof and cut his leg open. His misfortune benefitted me. The next weekend, at home to Wigan, I was named on the bench.

Midway through the first half, wearing the number 29 shirt and aged eighteen, I made my bow on the final weekend of the regular season as the last millennium came to an end. Wigan were still in their pomp, the reigning Super League champions with such as Gary Connolly, Kris Radlinski, Andy Farrell, Jason Robinson and Denis Betts in their ranks, superstars I'd grown up watching. I threw myself into it, managing to get a nice hit on Farrell. He picked himself up but, just before he played the ball, looked me straight in the eye and I knew it had hurt him. I felt ten feet tall.

It was a brutal introduction. We started well, leading when I came on, but a 38-point blitz in the second half restored normality. We gave it a good go but ran out of steam. Andy told me he was only going to put me on for ten minutes, but that I'd looked like I was enjoying myself so he left me out there. I think I played twenty-five and it was men against boys but was enough to see what I needed to do to get to that level. Call it luck, being in the right place and time to take advantage, but there's always an element of how you take the opportunity that presents itself and allow it to shape your destiny.

Afterwards, the players mingled in the bar at Belle Vue. I stood there with my orange juice, minding my own business, soaking it up, but also eavesdropping on the conversation of some of the Wigan lads. I heard Farrell ask: 'Who was that number 29?' There was a moment's pause, probably while someone looked up the teamsheet. 'Ellis,' they said. 'Gareth Ellis.'

'Mmm,' said Farrell. 'He's going to be some player.'

It's hard to describe what that felt like. I played alongside Andy for Great Britain some years later and, even then, was still in awe of him. I didn't react or say anything, just puffed my chest out a little bit and did even more in training the following day to make sure I could feel that way again.

We had spent most of the year struggling but, somehow, John managed to take the academy team on an end-of-season tour of Queensland. He wasn't just a visionary, but also someone that made things happen even in the toughest circumstances. I was, in truth, too old to be considered, but he decided to take me regardless. It was partly self-funded, which meant my parents helped me out yet again.

Dad dropped me off at the airport and, seeing my trepidation, Danny Brough reassured him that I'd be okay. "I'll make sure he doesn't get into any trouble," he said, which coming from Danny was pretty rich. I'll never forget the look on my dad's face.

To say I was a bit green would be an understatement. I hadn't even been on an aeroplane before and here I was, stopping off in Singapore, touching down in Darwin and then, via a small, local airline, Cairns, Townsville and Mackay, before we finally landed in Rockhampton. We stayed in a small beach town called Yeppoon, sleeping in dormitory accommodation. Eighteen or nineteen years old, we were having the adventure of our lives. Some lads might have snuck out of the dorm from time to time. I was too scared of John's wrath and, besides, that was never going to be my style.

We played the Central Queensland development team twice, the second game a curtain-raiser to a pre-season trial with Parramatta. David Solomona played for the Eels that day and, once again, in one of those peculiar twists of fate, he would become a teammate at Wakefield a few years later. We thoroughly enjoyed Australia. Years later some of that squad – Matty Wray, Andy Walker and Chris Feather – would end up emigrating and, of course, I had my own time there, as did Keith Mason. There's no doubt that the experience, when we were at our most impressionable had some bearing on those decisions.

We returned with Wakefield still in disarray and deducted two points for going into administration. I was breaking into the side around the same time as the John Pearman affair. He was an ex-city councillor who became chief executive, promising loads of money to rebuild the ground and team. Prior to signing my apprenticeship contract, the club showed me a model of their new stadium. It looked like something from *Thunderbirds*' Tracy Island, but never materialised. Another day, there was a reception in the city centre. All the players and staff were in attendance, and there were big piles of seafood on ice and free-flowing fizz. It seemed so exciting, like I was part of something that would be huge, but it was built on sand.

On the back of his vision and promises, Trinity signed a host of players for 2000: Martin Masella, Steve McNamara, Steve Prescott and Bobbie Goulding, after audacious bids for Jonah Lomu, Jason Robinson and Andrew Johns were turned down. Wakefield beat Leeds on the first weekend of the millennium campaign but that was as good as it got. By the end of May, the side was next to bottom and Andy Kelly was sacked. It was tough on him as he paid the price for high expectations. You have to build a team gradually, get the players playing as a group. And that takes time that Andy was never given.

Tony Kemp was a player I'd admired as a youngster when he was playing for Castleford. Now I found myself alongside him and, in June, he became my coach. A few weeks later, he gave me my full debut. It was at home to St Helens, I played centre and did enough to earn my place the following week. Tony had suggested, during an injury crisis, that I'd benefit from having a run in the threequarters. He told me it would benefit my development being a little further out from play and having to make some tough decisions, especially in terms of defensive reads. The temporary switch lasted more than two years but I loved it and it was, undoubtedly, an important part of my learning curve.

My career was beginning to take shape but, behind the scenes, all was not well. I can recall ferocious rows between players and staff when payments weren't coming through. You could sense turmoil, but I was living at home and, being on the lowest rung of the ladder, still got my own wage on time.

The club looked after us as youngsters, but meetings frequently descended into shouting matches. One of them became particularly heated at the end of July when we were sitting in the changing rooms underneath the function room a day before we were due to play Bradford. I'd heard rumours the first team players hadn't been paid. Now it had happened again and they were talking about refusing to take the field. It would have been a huge decision that would have thrown the club into disarray, but I couldn't blame them for standing up for themselves. Aged nineteen, I wasn't fully aware of how strongly my personality had been shaped by the impact of the Miners' Strike that had affected my family and our community, but I felt a strong bond with the players.

Tony spoke forcefully that we should go through with training and play our games, but not everyone agreed. Bobbie Goulding was particularly irate, calling out the lies that the players had been fed. Thankfully, a club official came into the room clutching a stack of brown envelopes. As they were handed out, there was a murmur of satisfaction around the room. I looked at mine, but felt guilty. As one of the younger guys on a low contract, I had still been getting paid each month. The older higher-salaried guys had been affected. I wasn't sure what to do. I nudged Franny Stephenson next to me and muttered: 'I've already been paid.' 'Shut up, son, and take the money,' he said, out of the side of his mouth. It was a bleak time. We got protected from the worst of it, but fair play to the senior boys. They kept their concerns pretty much sheltered from us.

In August, after just three months in the job, Kemp, dismayed at the way the players were treated, decided to quit. It was a shame. He was such an intelligent player and coach but never had a chance. As disappointed as I was for Tony, though, his departure led to John Harbin becoming head coach.

John's appointment could not have been better timed for me. He had been the main reason I'd progressed so quickly from academy to first team and now I'd be coached by him again. John's influence on me was so much more than that of a sports coach. The lessons he taught me then have influenced how I have conducted my life. 'Work hard, aim high, never take a shortcut...' is a message I'd later pass on to the younger players at Hull in my role as a coach there.

John had a big impact on how I conducted myself throughout my career. I've had a lot of coaches and there are three or four whose voices and messages have resonated most when times were at their toughest, spurring me on to be better.

It just goes to show that not everything is technical or tactical – no matter how good or respected you are at that. A lot of it in such a tough sport like rugby league is about mindset and wanting to compete and get the better of your opponent. Hunger.

As players continued to be unpaid, many drifted away from Trinity. It was a difficult time, but it could not have been better for a group of ex-academy lads desperate to make their mark.

5

Appreciation

THEY ARE GOOD PEOPLE, THE Ellises, generations of proud Yorkshire men and women with a strong sense of community.

Tom Ellis, my paternal grandfather, was in the Coldstream Guards during the Second World War. Afterwards, he became a bus driver who was always happy to drive the supporters' club coaches from Castleford to away games. A tall man, he played a bit of rugby league himself in his day but never saw me play the sport he loved, much to my dad's regret. It was from grandad Tom that the family obsession with rugby league came.

Tom could start an argument with anyone. Dad remembers how, when Cas were away at Hull, he'd go into the Threepenny Stand – the infamous terrace on which the most fervent Hull fans stood – with his Cas scarf on as if it were the most natural thing in the world.

He and Nana Doris lived in Allerton Bywater where they brought up five children. My dad had three sisters and a brother, Graham, who shared his obsession and would play for Lock Lane and then professionally with Doncaster and Hunslet.

After my grandad died, Doris moved into sheltered housing and we'd go there all the time, playing card games with her and my aunts, uncles and cousins. Nana wasn't particularly bothered about sport, but she became very interested in rugby league once I began to play professionally. She didn't come to watch but followed my career closely. Every fortnight, when she went to get her hair done, she would let everyone at the salon know all about 'our Gareth'.

I spent more time as a kid with mum's side of the family, although I never met my grandad, Frederick. Tragically, he was hit by a car and killed while he was in his fifties. After that, my Nana Mary and my mum's granny brought up five children and I spent most of my childhood with them, especially at auntie Jean's. She and uncle Roy had two boys, Matthew and Andrew, of a similar age to me and my younger sister Rachel, who was born in 1985. We spent much of the summer holidays staying over at each other's house. Nana Mary would often babysit and we soon realised we could wrap her around our little finger.

Mum and dad had four children. Lynsey was born in 1974, Joanne came along two years later and then I was born in May '81 – on Wembley weekend, to be precise. Mum was heavily pregnant and dad anxious at the prospect of leaving her while he went on his usual two-day bender to the Cup final with his mates from the Colliery. But mum wasn't due until the following week so she reassured him that all would be okay and off he went. There were no mobile phones back then and after a long day he rang to find that mum had gone into labour and it was too late for him to get home.

Dad was a miner and on 6 March 1984, along with thousands of other men across Yorkshire and the rest of the country, he went on strike. He stayed out until the very end, when he and most of his mates walked back to work almost a year later. He never really spoke much about it and I don't really remember it. I have a vague memory of a community hall where lots of men and women collected food and talked passionately in a way that I didn't understand but which I knew meant a great deal to them. It left an indelible mark.

Nowadays, I always find myself siding with the underdog, feeling solidarity with those who are standing up for themselves. For years, there were people dad wouldn't speak to because they had gone back to work early. His attitude mellowed and now he says that everyone had their own reasons for how they behaved. I can see the pride in his eyes that he stood fast with his mates and colleagues in support of what he believed in, though, and I am proud of him for that.

Dad initially started playing for Kippax, Fryston – alongside Sammy Lloyd and Steve Norton, who would both forge successful careers with Castleford and then Hull FC – and Castleford U19s. Then, along with his brother, Graham, he went to Lock Lane. He took me to a few games, but I can't honestly recall seeing him play.

He fondly recalls facing Wigan for Lock Lane in the Challenge Cup at Central Park. The tie was actually drawn at home, but the Cas amateurs agreed to switch it in exchange for a new kit. He was sidelined by a broken leg for a long time and on his return got signed by York, enjoying a few successful years with them. He played against the Australian touring team in 1978, one of his proudest moments. It's those memories you cherish and reminisce about irrespective of the standard you get to. In the early 1980s, he fell out with coach David Doyle-Davison and signed for Doncaster. It was there he played alongside Clive Sullivan for a season and took me to meet the great man as a toddler.

During the strike, the bit of money dad was getting from rugby must have been a great help. It was a hard time, but we were better off than most. He also had a great friendship with John Buckton, the Dons' stand-off. He still talks of the relationship they had on the field. If dad ever made a half-break or managed to poke his nose through a defensive line, he knew John would be there to off-load to and, more often than not, with John's speed it would end in a try. John delivered pies for a living and would give my dad anything left over which would have also been handy with a hungry family.

During the strike, dad played against Sheffield and did enough to impress Gary Hetherington, who was player-coach and owner of the Eagles then. Shortly after, Gary rang him to ask if he would be interested in signing for them. Unfortunately, Doncaster didn't want him to go and asked for £10,000, a big sum then. Eventually, a deal was done, Gary was very persuasive – as I would find out myself.

After the strike, the Selby coalfield was one of the few areas that seemed to offer any kind of future for Yorkshire miners. Dad started work at the Whitemoor pit and, when the National Coal Board began to incentivise families to move closer to it, he decided to take us to Bubwith, a village just a mile or so from where he worked. It was a fresh start and a new community after the trauma of it all. But after a few years, mum began to realise that village life wasn't really for her and eventually we moved to the bright lights of Selby.

Just to the right of our house was a patch of grass that made a perfect playing field, with two telegraph poles for rugby posts. Our neighbours Daniel Burton, Liam Pidcock, Paul McCarthy and I would spend hours kicking a football or rugby ball around.

By the time we moved to Selby, I was already in love with league and a huge Castleford fan. Dad first took me to Wheldon Road as a toddler, when I'd sit on a crash barrier at the railway end. Grandad Tom would have been with us in those early days.

I went to Flaxley Road Primary school where, aged around seven, I started playing organised rugby for the first time. Paul Ritson and a group of miners, dad included, set up a junior team, Whitemoor Warriors. We trained at the local high school and used the New Inn pub in Barlby as our base for club meetings and presentations. A key figure in setting it up and coaching the open age team was Vince Farrar, a revered ex-pro with Featherstone and Hull.

Despite its noble intentions, Whitemoor wasn't the most successful of clubs, we always struggled for players. At least I didn't have much competition for my place and ended up playing two seasons. It was there that I gained my first representative recognition, being chosen for Castleford and District and then Yorkshire U9s. I turned out at scrum-half and hooker, always in a scrum cap and shoulder pads too big for me. Often I'd play for the U9s, then change my shirt and go and appear for the U11s on the next field.

By the time I was nine, I had outgrown Whitemoor. Dad felt that if I was going to develop I needed to move, so he fixed me up at the Half Acres club in Castleford, which made sense given the amount of family we had living there. Andy Fowler was coach, old-school in his approach, so we were very well drilled.

It meant a lot of travelling for my dad, now a crane operator after taking redundancy at the pit. He'd dash home after work to pick me up before driving to Cas covered in grease and oil. I loved those journeys chatting away about anything, but rugby league mostly.

We did that for the best part of four years, picking up fish 'n' chips for tea from John's in Redhill or stopping by to see Nana Ellis, where she would fill us up with the best corned beef hash I have ever tasted.

Half Acres were much more successful than Whitemoor and felt like a proper club. They attracted kids from all over Cas and I played again for Yorkshire at U12s. The competitive streak was unusually strong in me, even at that age. I recall playing at Wheldon Road for Castleford schools against Oulton Raiders in a friendly and we were beating them easily. At a break in play, our coach, conscious that this was a big day for players on both sides, came onto the field and said: 'Their heads are down. Next time they get on our line, let them score.' I couldn't believe it. I actually remember being quite shocked and repeatedly pulled off tackles that prevented them.

Towards the end of the 1980s, Cas had a really strong team and, in 1988, signed the man who'd become my hero. In two seasons, Ronnie 'Rambo' Gibbs made a huge impression on the club and me in particular. I loved the fearless way he ran at opponents.

There used to be a pub in Castleford called The Ship Inn, a big, sprawling affair with loads of rooms. We were at a family birthday party there when I was eight and I was walking down the spiral staircase that was its centrepiece when I saw Ronnie coming towards me. I was star-struck. One of my dad's friends asked if he could sign something for me and he pulled out an autographed photo from his back pocket. That picture was stuck on my bedroom wall for years.

Years later, the pub was shut down and I somehow came to be the owner of one of the framed pictures that had hung on the wall. It showed Gibbs in action and that ended up in my bedroom as well. As an adult, I actually ran into him in Australia while I was playing for Wests Tigers and he was coaching a Queensland development team. I'd have loved to have spoken to him, but didn't have the nerve to introduce myself.

After four years at Half Acres, word went around that our team would fold. Amid the uncertainty and toll that constant travelling had taken on my dad and family, I decided to stop playing rugby altogether. At the time, one of my best friends, Richard Pennistone, was playing for a football team called H&R Selby, based near the old Tate & Lyle plant on the outskirts of town. I decided to join him and for a year or so, played in midfield most Saturdays in a local league. I was really into football around that time. As a kid, I'd supported Liverpool but, by my teens, I was looking for another side and as my dad had a soft spot for Sheffield Wednesday, they became my team. They were really good in the 1990s, regularly reaching finals and finishing in the top half of the Premier League, Carlton Palmer, John Sheridan, Chris Bart-Williams and Chris Woods my new heroes. Dad took me to a home game for my birthday and I was in awe of the noise and atmosphere at Hillsborough.

I carried on playing some rugby league thanks to our PE teacher, Mr Simpson, who played briefly for Hunslet and London. He started a team at Selby High. He would often take me to train with the York schools' side after lessons, for which I was incredibly grateful. After two years I went back to Half Acres. Mick Mallinson was running the team then, a fantastic coach who'd do anything for the lads. Each year, we'd get new kit sponsored by local businesses and training gear. He encouraged us to spend time together after training.

I became part of the U16s, who played on a field at the back of Castleford baths. The pitch was on a big slope, but over the season we mastered it. We'd get teams into the bottom corner and tackle them to death so they couldn't get out. After two seasons Half Acres folded, so at the end of 1997 we all decamped to Lock Lane.

At first, we were based at the Early Bath on Wheldon Road, just across from the Castleford ground, which was a primitive affair. At the back of the pub were changing rooms and a big old-fashioned bath that was absolutely disgusting. You jumped in it and came out dirtier, but it kept us grounded. After a game, they would bring the food out for all the teams and it always seemed to be beef dripping sandwiches. I never touched them. Later, we moved closer to our pitch at the Britannia pub where I would spend hours after matches eating packets of Bacon Fries and playing 'Killer' on the pool table with teammates like Wally, who did his best to entertain the entire pub egged on by members of the first team. Craig Poskitt would host a weekly game of *Play Your Cards Right* which went on for ages and kept everyone in there long enough for the committee members to do repeated rounds of the place selling lotto tickets.

By the time we were sixteen, we started going into town on a Saturday night. We knew which pubs would turn a blind eye and let us in and would often end the night in 'Legends' nightclub. John Hambleton had become my best mate and his parents' house in Castleford was my second home. I spent most weekends there and got to know his mum and dad, Lynn and Steve, really well too.

Having done okay in my GCSEs, I enrolled at Selby College studying a BTEC Diploma in Public Services but still with no idea of what I was going to do, in danger of taking the first job that came along whether I liked it or not. I had little motivation for studying and spent my first year at college drifting between lessons. In my second, I became more focused. Towards the end of the course, in the spring of 1999, I applied for a number of apprenticeships, including one with British Aerospace at Church Fenton. I had to do a test as part of the recruitment process and took it very seriously. I pored over each question, taking my time, thinking hard about the answers before carefully writing down what I thought would be the correct response. Before I knew it the test was over and I was barely half way through. Needless to say, I didn't get it but learned a little about myself. I work slowly and methodically, like to get things right and will take my time to do any task. I call it having an eye for detail.

When I think about what my dad did for me, it's not until now that I appreciate that level of commitment and sacrifices my parents made. When I did finally retire as a rugby league player, one of the proudest moments was dad thanking me for the journey he'd been on through my exploits. That's the only repayment you can give for those early years of traipsing everywhere. Dad has been with me all the way and was proud as punch when I followed in his footsteps.

Once at Wakefield, despite the difficult times, we had fun during my early years. I spent time living with quite a few teammates but, at the start, actually lived for a few months in a Portakabin there.

Belle Vue was a ramshackle ground with odd bits of grandstand and terracing thrown together over the years. There were a few old hospitality boxes which Steve Snitch, who came over from Hull, had realised were never in use. He checked with the club and we moved in. We bought a bit of furniture from some second hand stores, fitted beds and installed a microwave and, before we knew it, Snitchy and I were the proud inhabitants of two adjoining bachelor pads. Some of our teammates would even crash with us. My mum and dad came to visit – once. Having to walk across the pitch in the dark, the only company being 'Rat' the nightwatchman and his terrifying Alsatian, was enough for them.

After a few months, I'd also had enough and, having passed my driving test and bought my first car, moved home again for a while. I'd become best mates with Tom Haughey and Chris Feather, so we moved in together. We had a great place just on the outskirts of Wakefield. It was ideal for parties and there was a lawn out front where we would have barbecues and play croquet, of all things.

Rugby league was also how I met my wife, Rachael. We may never have got together were it not for referee Phil Bentham being so picky over a pitch inspection.

It was a cold Friday night in late February 2006, when Castleford came to Headingley. There was frost on the ground but still every chance that the game would be played. The supporters had already started to come in, but Phil wasn't happy about a frozen patch in front of the South Stand and, less than two hours before kick-off, he called it off. Leeds were desperate to get the game played as soon as possible, so it was swiftly re-scheduled for the Sunday.

The postponement was inconvenient especially for commercial sponsors, one of whom, Gary Kilmartin, had invited his friends, Carol and Stuart Roberts. When the match was rearranged, Carol couldn't make it so Stuart invited his daughter, Rachael, instead. I wasn't due to play anyway. I was out with a knee injury, which meant that I was on corporate duty and in the main sponsors' room when my eyes fell on Rachael and I was instantly reminded of a previous meeting with her. We smiled at one another but didn't speak.

A few weeks earlier, I had been on a night out in Leeds city centre with some of the lads when I bumped into her in a bar. We chatted for a while and, before we parted, I asked for her telephone number.

For some reason I didn't have my phone with me, so I asked Chris Feather to put her number into his. He then rang her so that she had his number, but neither of us followed it up until we saw each other again at Headingley. Not long after we had spotted each other a second time, Chris rang me and said someone has sent you a message on my phone. A few days later, I picked Rachael up at her home and we went for a drink together in York.

In those early days, it wasn't always easy for us to spend time together. She lived an hour away but, conveniently, worked in Leeds so after training I would often head into town and pick her up when she finished. Our relationship moved forward quickly. Each time she stayed, she brought clothes in an overnight bag and I noticed that she wasn't taking much of it back again. Before I knew it, she had a couple of drawers, most of my wardrobe and a shelf in the bathroom full of her stuff.

Before I met Rachael, I had never really had a steady girlfriend and grown used to organising my own life. But, like most couples, you tend to focus on the things you do best and Rachael is a planner who, gradually, started to organise me. Even in those early days, she had little to do with my rugby career. She always asked if I'd won and came to a few games, but that was the extent of her interest and it suited me fine.

We both enjoyed travelling to new places. At the end of the 2006 season, I went on tour with Great Britain and she flew out to meet me in Australia as it came to an end. From there, we went on our first holiday together, to Thailand. Because my flights had been paid for by the RFL, I flew home in business class, Rachael in economy. I promised to try and get her upgraded but unfortunately they wouldn't allow it so the next best thing I could do was offer to swap seats. I gallantly told her that, once the plane was in the air, we'd change. Within seconds of the 'seatbelts off' sign lighting up, she appeared in the business class cabin only to find me fast asleep.

It was during 2007 that we began to explore the possibility of moving to Australia. She had backpacked there, living out of hostels and working in nightclubs, and loved it. The subsequent move was idyllic and felt like the perfect time to start a family. It wasn't too long before Rachael fell pregnant and we looked forward blissfully to the arrival of our first child. But the spell was broken when Rachael had a miscarriage.

It was heartbreaking and, knowing how close she is to her family, I was surprised she didn't want to go home. Going through that experience makes you feel very vulnerable but we found, in telling people what had happened, that we weren't alone – the Troddens and O'Neills were a great comfort. So many other couples told us that they too had had the same experience and had then had successful pregnancies later on. It reassured us and, within a few months, Rachael was pregnant once again.

I decided to make an honest woman of her and in the middle of the 2009 season I had a few days off, so we took the opportunity to see more of Australia. We flew north and spent time on Hamilton Island, part of the Whitsundays, just off the Queensland coast. It was beautiful, white sandy beaches and crystal clear waters. The only mode of transport was a golf buggy, so we hired one and drove to a look-out called One Tree Hill, where I hoped to pop the question. I imagined finding a quiet spot overlooking the water, where I would get down on one knee. But when we arrived the place was packed. We wandered around and, having seen everything there was to see, Rachael suggested we head back to town. She could see I was up to something as I fumbled around trying to find more things for us to do until the crowds dispersed. Eventually they went away and I was able to pluck up the courage.

When our first-born Isaac finally arrived, I was overcome with emotion. Trying to blink away the tears, I struggled to find the best way to hold him in my big, clumsy hands. The first night in our apartment was carnage. Knowing that mother and son were coming home, I tried to cook a nice meal for us to enjoy once Isaac was asleep. But a crying baby and a tired and fractious wife meant it all ended in tears. I should have just bought a takeaway.

It was nice to know people were there for us if we needed them, but we were largely left to ourselves and it was a few months before the grandparents came out to see us and Isaac. Over the next few years we became more and more convinced that we didn't want him growing up on the opposite side of the world to his family, although when he is old enough to know what a fantastic place Sydney is, he may not thank us for that.

Eva came along when we were back settled in Wetherby and is very much like me, a little introverted and often shy. Sometimes I get frustrated when she clings to me or Rachael when we try to drop her off at school, but then I think of myself and what I was like as a kid. On the flip side, she can be hilarious at home and, as soon as any music comes on, she's up on her feet dancing around the house, doing cartwheels across the living room and pulling silly faces at the same time. She clearly gets that from her mother.

Florence arrived just before Christmas 2016 and we eventually moved to Bubwith, the small village where I used to live as a kid when my dad moved to work at Whitemoor Colliery.

Each of our kids is different. Isaac is very laid back, but knows his own mind. He loves his football and was awarded player of the year for North Duffield Dragons U13s. Recently, he has taken an interest in rugby union with Selby and won their Most Improved Player award. To say he hasn't been playing long, he has really taken to it and enjoys the contact. Sounds familiar. He is studious, taking his time with things with a quiet determination to give of his best and is the same on the football field.

Eva is a worrier and Florence is probably a typical third child, a bit wilder than the others, who has to work hard to find her place in the family, but who has no trouble holding her own.

I treasure the time that I get to share with them.

6

Leadership

I WAS IN AND OUT of the Wakefield side in 2001 but, when not in the first team, earned my stripes and improved my game with the 'A' team. I loved playing in the reserves. It's hard for me to imagine how I would have ever become a full-time professional were it not for the progress I made on those Thursday nights under Johnny Thompson. Through my performances and growing reputation, first team chances came around more frequently. By the middle of the season I was picked every week, which led to another rite of passage.

At training, the first team used the home changing rooms while the apprentices were consigned to the away ones, smaller and older, packed with old kit and an ancient tiled bath. Arriving one Tuesday night I headed as usual for the apprentices' room, until Gary Price and Andy Fisher called out to me to join them. That was it, I would be a first team player for the next twenty years.

It was a tough year for Wakefield, but we never feared relegation until the very end. Huddersfield had spent all season bottom of the league but, in the last few months, began to pick up points, gradually closing the gap. We had a chance in the penultimate round to beat them at our own ground and consign them to the drop but blew it, losing to a late try and so went into the last weekend just a point ahead. Huddersfield hosted London and we were away at Salford and needed to win to stay up.

The atmosphere was electric as the City Reds built up an 18-14 lead by half-time. We were six points down as the game went into the final ten minutes. Urged on by a noisy crowd, tempers began to fray and Salford went down to 12 men, Stuart Littler sent off for a trip on Martin Pearson. Bobbie Goulding, then with our opponents and still owed money by Wakefield, was desperate to see us relegated and looked to have done so when he intercepted to score. But the ref pulled him up for being deliberately offside and then sin-binned him for it. Goulding was fuming and completely lost it when Justin Brooker threw the ball at him. That led to a mass brawl, all of us piling in. When it calmed down, Goulding was shown a red card, as was Brooker.

With Salford down to 11 men, we threw the ball around looking for the winning try which came, amid incredible celebrations from our fans, from Neil Law. Paul March scored again in stoppage time and, as the hooter went, supporters poured onto the field. It was like winning a Grand Final, I can still see myself celebrating between the posts. It was an unbelievable moment, everything had conspired against us that season but, finally, we had survived. We were still unsure whether we would be allowed to play in Super League in 2002 if our ground failed to meet their minimum standards but, for now, that didn't matter. We just wanted to celebrate. I often wonder what would have become of my career if we had taken the drop.

For John Harbin, it had all been too much. I had never seen a man put so much of himself into a group of players. He took the responsibility of keeping Wakefield in Super League personally and it took its toll on his health. Soon after it was confirmed that we would be staying up, he left the club.

He showed that he was much more than just a rugby league coach when he made his next move into professional football, as fitness conditioner and sports psychologist at Oldham Athletic, alongside Iain Dowie. He then followed Dowie around the country to Crystal Palace, Charlton, Coventry and QPR. After a brief spell at Swansea, he moved back to Queensland and was successful again in his return to league. A few years later he was back in England with Plymouth, Port Vale, Northampton and back to Oldham.

Guided by John's hand, my career was about to take off and go into overdrive. After he left, a clutch of players followed him. Danny Brough and Paul March were allowed to go, Willie Poching went to Leeds, Ryan Hudson signed for Castleford and Keith Mason moved to Melbourne. With so many departures, I expected to be a regular but the new coach, Peter Roe, saw it differently. I started the next season on the bench for the opening Challenge Cup rounds. I hid my disappointment, turning up earlier for training and staying later. Within weeks I was back in the starting line-up and never looked back. It was during this time that I became more independent in how I prepared for games and training.

It was yet another tough year for Wakefield, but one in which my performances really came to the fore. For the first time I was feeling a responsibility to play well to give us a chance of victory. Picking up the man of the match award in a losing performance became a regular event. I got stronger every week, sensing other players feeling my presence, which motivated me in training. I gave every drill, every lift, a purpose by relating it to a specific action on the field.

In July, Roe was sacked and Shane McNally was appointed as temporary coach, Adrian Vowles as his assistant. Shane, in many ways, was similar to John, a typically hard-nosed Queenslander who liked what he saw in me in terms of my work ethic. We snatched enough points in the final ten games to drag us off bottom, beating Warrington on the last day keeping us up and sending Salford down.

Going into the pack, as happened more frequently in the second half of the 2002 season, was the smartest thing I ever did. If I had continued to play centre, I'd have been found out eventually. I wasn't fast enough, didn't have the range of skills that position demands. Even so, the times I played there for Wakefield helped me no end.

Those close calls, with our livelihoods at stake, very much bred an 'us and them' mentality which brought the team together. It made us tight as a group – probably one of the most united I've been involved with – and when it really mattered we were able to dig in, especially when survival was at stake. Some of those are still the biggest games of my career, not least because they meant so much to so many people.

Shane was the one that really encouraged me to kick on and find something extra, making me realise the qualities I could bring to the team. He even engineered a move to stand-off for a while as he thought it would benefit the side if I could get my hands on the ball more and influence the game as much as I could.

The following year, he asked my thoughts on making me captain at Wakefield, at the age of 21. My initial reaction was 'no chance'. It had taken me two years even to speak in that environment and now I was being asked to lead the team. My vision of the role was that it was someone's who shouted and bawled, told everyone what to do and ruled the roost. But what Shane said to me – and it was the first time anyone had – was that I didn't realise how much my work ethic and standing within the team influenced the other players.

That came as a real shock. I just saw myself as someone who battled away doing what they had to and it took a bit of persuasion for me to give the armband a go. I had much to learn, but some good guys around me who guided and helped. It was the first indication I might have a brighter future than I thought. The only pressure was from me, to feel I earned my stripes, which remained my motivation. But with success came something I've never enjoyed: the limelight. It gave me a public profile I never wanted and have only grudgingly tolerated since. My first brush with 'celebrity' was on nights out in Wakefield with fellow apprentices starting to break into the first team. We would rock up to a nightclub and jump to the front of the queue, because someone knew the bouncer. Other punters would nudge themselves and point us out and I would hate it.

During 2002, I'd won a few man of the match awards which led to one of my worst nightmares – speaking in public. I found that daunting and relied on the most awful clichés for years. I'd like to think I've always done the right thing when asked for an autograph or photo. We had a sign on the wall at the training ground at Hull which said: 'A moment for you can be a lifetime of memories.' It reminded us of the huge role we play in supporters' experiences.

I was never comfortable with being captain, even at Hull. I always found it a real challenge. There are some days, going into any work environment, when you don't want to be happy. You need a rant and a moan. Well, as captain you can't afford to do it. You can't ever have an off day if you are setting a lead. You had to paint the smile on, no matter how sore or broken you felt.

In Australia, the media intrusion was worse and just wasn't for me. You've got a platform to be in the spotlight if you choose there. Every channel has TV shows featuring the players, but that's not me. I prefer to stay in the background, doing what's expected of me and minding my own business.

Once, at Wests Tigers, we were playing the Roosters in the play-offs, an epic encounter. I got put on report for a high tackle on Todd Carney. We had a swimming session the following day and as I got out my car to go to the open air pool, a host of cameramen ran towards me. Microphones were poked in my face. Was I worried about missing facing Canberra the following week? That stuff unsettled me more than any prospect of a ban.

I had been a regular in the Wakefield side for four seasons and we'd never finished higher than tenth in the league. There had been a bit of interest in me during 2003, but it never came to anything, largely because of my own reluctance to push for a move.

7

A Representative

IN NOVEMBER 2002, I WAS heading down under again, having been selected by the England Knights for a three-match tour of Fiji and Tonga. It was the representative level below the full Great Britain side, made up of the cream of Super League's younger players. Just as I got my debut for Wakefield due to someone's misfortune, I was only selected because another player missed a squad meeting.

We set up base in Manly before jetting off for Fiji, who we played twice. We beat them easily in the first game in Nadi then moved to Suva, the capital, for the second. It was farcical. Beforehand, it had poured down and frogs were jumping all over the pitch. The Fiji officials had decided they must win at all costs so brought in a referee who was going to make absolutely certain that would happen.

From the first few minutes, we were pulled up for everything ... offside, laying on, forward passes. It was massively frustrating to a bunch of young guys who really wanted to do well in their country's shirt. We just about managed to keep our heads but John Kear, our manager, was raging. At one point, it looked like he would pull us off the pitch. I think it was only the fear of what the repercussions might be that stopped him from doing so.

Nevertheless, the experience was incredible and I loved working with John. His man-management of young blokes away from home for three weeks was fantastic. At the end of the tour, there was a celebration event and I was given the award for Player of the Tour, which was totally unexpected given the likes of Andy Lynch, Danny McGuire, Rob Burrow and Sean O'Loughlin were also in that squad.

That was the first time it started to hit home that I could do something out of the ordinary. My confidence was growing and I began to feel my desire for success might outstrip my club's potential. It was a sentiment reinforced when, a few weeks later, I was chosen as Wakefield's representative in the England squad for the World Sevens tournament in Sydney and so, shortly before the start of the 2003 season, I was on a plane back to Australia.

We were only there for a week or so, and the tournament itself lasted no more than a long weekend, but it was another special trip alongside some of the best players in the world representing 24 different club and international teams.

England, coached by the late Mike Gregory and with Phil Clarke as team manager, included the likes of Andy Farrell, Richard Horne, Danny Orr, Lee Gilmour, Marcus St Hilaire and a sensational Keith Senior, who looked after me. We scored tries for fun on the first day, beating Tonga and an Aboriginal team. Those wins earned us a place in the quarter-finals against France the next day. There was a decent crowd building as we beat them 30-10 and then overcame Manly in the semis. We went into the final confident that we could beat Brian Smith's Parramatta, but they came out flying, scoring five tries in the first half to effectively kill off the game.

On returning home, my performances for Wakefield were solid enough to be called up for my only appearance for Yorkshire, which turned out to be the last-ever War of the Roses game against Lancashire. I turned up to camp in Leeds on Wednesday for the game, at Odsal, on the Friday. Graham Steadman was coach and given the short time we had together keen to build team spirit. The first thing he did was to say it was compulsory to go out drinking around Pontefract, presumably so he didn't have to pay for a taxi home. I remember thinking that wasn't how I expected elite rugby to be, but it was great fun and it worked because, a few days later, we hammered them. Sadly, there weren't many supporters there and I can't say it was much of a career highlight, but it was nice to be recognised again at that stage of my career.

I have always been a big advocate for the Roses contest – a fixture I grew up watching – and having seen the intensity of State of Origin would love to see it flourish. Truth is, though, the game was a damp squib. I still think it's a great concept but what we are guilty of doing in the game is trying things and, when they are not as big as we want them to be, moving on rather than waiting for them to develop.

In Australia, I was told that Origin wasn't that significant at the start. It's just grown over a period of time, the rivalry exploited to a point where it's now one of the most anticipated events in the calendar. It's something you get behind regardless of whether you even take an interest in the sport.

In October the following year, I was piling my golf clubs into my boot after a round with my mate, John Hambleton, when my mobile rang. It was Shane McNally. 'I've just come off the phone with David Waite,' he said. 'You're in the Great Britain squad; he's picked you to play against Australia. Well done, mate.' Shane carried on talking but I don't think I heard any of it. I had to wait until I bought a paper the next day to confirm that I was in the squad for the Ashes Series, almost aghast at seeing my name. Then I got an official letter in the post from the RFL. It had all happened in the space of about five years since playing for Lock Lane and was a bit overwhelming.

The Great Britain team has always meant a great deal to me. As a kid, I remembered watching the brilliant Ashes Series of the early 1990s and will never forget going to London to see the Lions beat the Aussies at Wembley in 1994. I had never witnessed anything like it, union jacks everywhere and followers of all the clubs mingling in support of the national side.

In 2019, I was as keen as anyone when the GB brand was re-formed for a tour to New Zealand and Papua New Guinea and just as devastated and embarrassed when the Lions were beaten in all four games. I couldn't understand how the squad and coaching team could've been so badly prepared, turned over with such little fight.

But back to 2003, and there was still a part of me that thought I was going to get turned away when I arrived at the Radisson Hotel, near Manchester Airport. Dad dropped me off, no tears this time, but still some anxiety that I might have left something behind. We were flying to Spain the next day to go into camp and I must have checked my passport was in my bag a dozen times.

I roomed with Kris Radlinski and still remember the butterflies inside. He was really friendly but I was in awe of him, desperate to learn anything I could about how he prepared, watching how he went about his business, trying to pick up any tips.

At dinner, then breakfast and in the team meetings, I tried to stay calm and be myself, but I was unbelievably nervous. Everywhere I looked there were these icons of the game... Andy Farrell, Adrian Morley, Barrie McDermott, Keith Senior. Kevin Sinfield was the same age as me but far more self-assured. He had been around the international setup and had plenty of his teammates in the squad. I didn't really know anyone. Not only was this my first call-up, but I was the only player from Wakefield.

I found it really difficult to be at ease with myself. I had always been shy, but I was worried it might be interpreted as being arrogant or aloof. I wanted so much to chat away confidently, but I couldn't say anything in case it came out stupid; it felt like torture initially. Gradually, some of my new teammates found the time to chat with me, Paul Sculthorpe, Kevin, Barrie and Keith especially, and that helped me to relax a bit. Over time and greater understanding, that nervousness and anxiety tended to bring the best out of me.

I presumed I was only in the squad for experience, unlikely to play in any of the games, which was fine. I was just wanted to justify my selection. We trained every day in Malaga, although nothing too strenuous. The main objective was to build a team spirit. I had been surprised to see some of the lads had brought golf clubs along and I kind of wished I had taken mine. Each day after training there was an activity that brought us together and one day we went to Puerto Banus for a meal and a few drinks. Phil Clarke was in charge of the RFL credit card and a few of the boys went to town and ordered lobster, which was a bit of an eye-opener when the bill arrived.

I soon recognised that this group were much like us at Wakefield. Some didn't drink, others had a few, and others had more than a few, yet you wouldn't have noticed it next day on the training field.

Back in England, we had a few days off before we met up again at the Marriott hotel at Worsley, which was to become our home for the next four weeks. We were kept busy and that suited me, meaning less time to feel awkward and self-conscious. After breakfast each day, our bus would drop us off at Sale Sharks' training ground. The squad was split in two, those likely to feature in the Test and those not. The Test lads were treated like kings, their workload carefully managed, diet and nutrition a priority. The rest of us became fodder for them, a supporting cast, re-creating plays the opposition were likely to put on or mimicking traits of certain individuals, so how to defend against them could be practised.

That would then be followed by an absolute beasting from the team conditioner, Carl Jennings, designed to keep us in shape should we be called upon. Meanwhile, the likes of Morley and Farrell would look on with amusement, sipping protein shakes before going for a rub-down and a game of poker! I saw such torture as a chance to show what I could do. Harder the drills, the more I could stand out.

This Ashes Series would be the last played between Great Britain and Australia. Three games over successive weekends caught the imagination of the players and supporters and tickets sold well. The Kangaroos were going through a bit of transition while we had lads in our side at the peak of their careers. There was real belief that for the first time in nearly three decades we could beat them. Even I could feel it as we set off for Wigan for the opening encounter.

That optimism lasted about eleven seconds. That's how long it took for Adrian Morley to hunt down Robbie Kearns from the kick off and flatten him. We had sensed that Moz was wound up for this. He played his rugby in Australia for Sydney Roosters and we had seen in training that he couldn't wait to get stuck into the Aussies.

Steve Ganson showed him the red card and we faced the prospect of playing the best team in the world for over 79 minutes with 12 men. I felt sorry for Moz, couldn't help thinking that a sending-off wouldn't have occurred if this had been an Aussie referee faced with

I grew up a Castleford fan, *left*, and was a regular at Wheldon Road with my mates in the late 1980s.

Wearing a Brisbane Broncos shirt, *right*, brought back by my uncle from the 1988 Ashes tour.

Below: I enjoyed playing football too, lining up for Selby High School U12s.

At the age of 17, *left and above*, I was almost ready to break into Lock Lane's first team, carrying on a family tradition, until Wakefield Trinity called.

Enjoying 'Mad Monday', *left*, with my Wakefield teammates in 2001.

My first playing trip overseas was a Pacific tour with England Knights in 2002 – a fabulous experience. Our Test match with Fiji, *above*, followed a torrential downpour. Some of us chose to watch one game from the media box, *right*.

Left: Lining up with Jamie Peacock and Paul Wellens before my Test debut against Australia in 2003.

Above: Finally, in 2007, I got my hands on this beauty.

Above: After four years at Wakefield, I signed for Leeds.

Right: During the 2004 Tri Nations series. I was so disappointed to be left out of the final.

Below: My name is immortalised forever.

Above: Christmas Day in Australia in 2008 was definitely a strange experience for Rachael and me.

Above: When dad landed in Sydney for the 2010 play-offs, he was met by his new grandson and the *Sydney Telegraph*.

Left: Training with Benji Marshall, who became – and still is – one of my best mates.

Above: Going in for a try for Wests Tigers against Canberra Raiders.

Left: Following on from – and catching up with – Garry Schofield and Ellery Hanley, who had been legends at Balmain back in the 1980s.

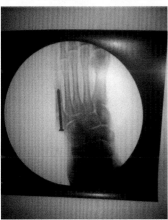

Left: Who'd have thought that one small bone could cause so much damage and heartache?

Right: In 2020, I spent a night in hospital after a head injury caused by a clash of heads.

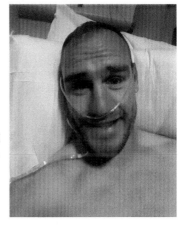

Above: There's nothing like a winner's dressing room – here I am pictured with three Hull teammates, Kirk Yeaman, Fetuli Talanoa and Carlos Tuimavave in 2016.

Above: The first Hull FC captain to lift the Challenge Cup at Wembley – my happiest moment in the game. Our tackle machine hero Danny Houghton enjoyed it too.

Left: An open top bus ride following our 2016 Cup final win. *Inset*: More celebrations in Hull – the Queen's Gardens packed with thousands of FC fans.

Pictured above: John Harbin discovered and nurtured my potential at Wakefield and remains a good friend.

Left: Mum and dad join me at the KC Stadium.

Above left: Lifting the Cup on the Town Hall balcony had been a dream ever since seeing John Joyner do it for Castleford in 1986. *Right*: Showing the Cup off to my sisters and Rachael.

Clockwise from top: Daughter Eva wears my medal; Eldest Isaac helps me celebrate; youngest Florence tries it on for size; and I bump into myself at Wembley Stadium!

the prospect of dismissing one of his own. Despite that disadvantage, I witnessed a heroic performance from my new teammates and with just eight minutes left, we were ahead 18-14. An almost miraculous victory was on the cards, but that reckoned without Darren Lockyer who set up and scored the winner.

Given how we'd played, there was a lot of belief in the days that followed. The same routine followed ahead of the Second Test in Hull. The KC Stadium was packed and for this occasion I was on pitchside duty having been promoted to water carrier. A dozen times or more I was on the field, close to the action, as we raced to a 20-8 lead inside the first twenty minutes. We were brilliant. It seemed all that optimism had been well founded. Inevitably, though, Australia clawed their way back and I could sense the lads getting frustrated. Heading into the final ten minutes it was 20-20. We missed an opportunity to knock over a drop-goal, they didn't, and that was it, another late loss.

With the series gone, the atmosphere in our dressing room was bleak. I was intrigued to see how the senior players would respond and what they'd say and do to lift themselves and their teammates. The mood stayed low for the rest of the night but, by next morning, it had changed. Everyone was talking about avoiding a whitewash. Nobody had really spoken to alter the spirits, it was just a collective refocusing led by David Waite and the senior guys to find a new goal.

There was talk that Waite might use the final Test to have a look at a few other lads, to give as many people as possible a chance, but I never got too carried away by that. I've found that, in any team I've been involved in, there's always someone who wants to shortcut their way into being respected by being class clown. The higher I've gone in the game the less tolerance there is. He might be a good laugh on a night out, but when it boils down to it you want the guy who has been taking things seriously alongside you rather than the joker.

I continued to train as hard as I could and after a team meeting assistant coach Graham Steadman came up. As the rest of the team drifted away, he said quietly: 'If he asks if you can play prop, say yes.'

On Wednesday morning I was pulled into some of the forward work. David was also taking more time with me, giving me bits of advice. 'If you find yourself in this position, do that,' he'd say. It was same again on Thursday; I trained with the 'probables' as opposed to 'hopefuls' and left the session feeling I was part of the GB pack.

Waite told me I would be on the bench. The following night, after our evening meal, we gathered in the team room, chairs laid out in rows. David spoke about the importance of the Third Test, what he wanted us to do and proceeded to announce the team. One by one, each player was called up to the front and presented with their match shirt to applause from the group. Finally: 'Number 17, Gareth Ellis'. I was also presented with my first cap. As I sat back in my seat, I couldn't take my eyes off either of them.

As I've grown older, I've become more fascinated with the idea of being a custodian. I find the heritage numbers employed by many clubs a great idea. I can feel history in the shirt, number or role. Back in 2003, I wouldn't have been able to articulate it very well, but I like to think I understood the responsibility and could not have been prouder or happier. There was still time for the Ellis clan to mobilise themselves now that my selection was confirmed. Dad was joined by my mum, sisters and several of my aunties, uncles and cousins.

Walking into the dressing room, I saw that shirt hung up for me and cradled it. Thirty minutes before warm-up, the mood changed. Nobody gave a signal, it just happened. Someone turned the music off and the joking came to an end. I'm quiet. I hadn't earned the right to say anything yet and so just listened.

I caught sight of myself in a mirror, lingering for a while, enjoying the image in that famous white chevroned shirt. Some lads had their training gear on for the warm-up, not me. I didn't want anything to cover it up. Back inside, there were some final words and then we were outside again, walking onto the pitch alongside the Aussies and hearing the roar of the crowd. I belted out the national anthem but it was the sense of standing there, arms slung around the shoulders of my teammates that I enjoyed the most, ready to go into battle.

My chance came earlier than I imagined. I was on in the first half. If anyone paid close attention to my movements and performance in those first few minutes of my debut, they'd have seen me running around like a headless chicken, over-excited, legs like jelly, timing totally amiss, trying too hard to impress. I was just desperate to do something to get me into the game, make a run, tackle, pass, settle myself down, something to make me feel like I was meant to be there. After thirty seconds or so I was second man into a tackle, then making another. Soon enough, I had the ball in my hand. I took it cleanly and ran it in hard then made a quick play the ball. That did the trick. I was a Great Britain player.

It was another close game. With three minutes left, we led 12-6. It looked like I would mark my debut with a win. But that reckoned without yet another Aussie late show. The difference between the teams throughout the series had been slim, but Australia had Darren Lockyer and he was it. There were some really disappointed guys in that dressing room. To see Moz and Faz absolutely devastated made an impression on me. I left no real mark on the game. The reports next day made no mention of my name and, while I'd tried to savour the moment, I can't recall much about the action but did resolve to do everything I could to ensure I wouldn't be a 'one-cap wonder'.

That final Test was the only one I played for David Waite. He was a very deep thinker, a serious man. I had a few conversations with him during the month or so in camp, but we only ever spoke about rugby. He gave the impression that the sport totally consumed him.

David placed a great importance on the mental side of the game and had us doing all sorts of things to emphasise the importance of positive thinking such as walking over hot coals and trying to punch our way through pieces of wood. I've always been open to new ideas so found it interesting and entertaining. But when it came to his turn to break a plank, he just couldn't do it. As each attempt failed he got more and more frustrated, much to the amusement of the group.

The player with the biggest influence around the camp was, without doubt, Andy Farrell. He had a real aura. I never approached him, asked for help or engaged him in conversation; he was an intimidating figure for sure. On and off the field he was very vocal, which added to that sense of being someone not to mess with. He demanded a lot and let you know if he felt you hadn't measured up.

The time I spent in the GB camp certainly left an impression. It opened my eyes to what rugby league was really all about. I had lived in my Wakefield bubble and grown used to the way things were at Trinity. I was accustomed to life at a club that had no real training base, where we'd get no training kit until Christmas, used to making do. I loved the club and everyone associated with it. They set me on my way. Internationals were another world and I realised that, for the likes of Farrell, Paul Sculthorpe and Kevin Sinfield, this was the norm. This is what club rugby league looks like when you play for Wigan, Saints or Leeds.

8

Headingley Bound

I BEGAN TO FEEL THAT this was as good as it was going to get at Wakefield. The club had looked after me, each year my contract had been improved and I was now an established member of the side. I was still unsure of my best position, but wasn't particularly bothered.

The 2004 season was one of my best and most enjoyable years. The Great Britain experience gave me a huge amount of confidence and self-belief that I took into pre-season training. Plus, we had the likes of Sid Domic, Jason Demetriou, David Solomona, Ben Jeffries, Jamie Rooney and Michael Korkidas in the side.

Being captain also made me step up. All those experienced guys didn't see it as a chance to take advantage of my inexperience in the role but really supported me. It's no surprise that Jason became a top NRL head coach, nor that we were competitive throughout and reached the play-offs for the first time in the summer era. All year, Shane encouraged me to be as involved as possible and I spent a lot of time playing stand-off and loose forward. I also watched hours of video tapes, so many times I probably wore them out.

As the season ticked over, we grew in confidence on the back of big wins against the likes of Castleford and St Helens. Mid-summer, we had climbed to eighth in the league and another string of wins meant that we comfortably qualified for the post-season.

We had to travel to Hull in the opening week of the play-offs, but I was struggling. A few weeks earlier, I'd picked up an ankle ligament injury at Huddersfield, which made it unstable and excruciatingly painful. Normally it would have meant an operation, but I had it jabbed, strapped up and played on. We scored four second-half tries to win 28-18, the only thing I recall being my emergence out of the line to tip the ball on to Chris Feather, who crashed over out wide. As I jumped on him to give him a massive hug, I landed on my ankle and was in agony, but we had won and next up were Wigan.

We went into that game hopeful, but not expectant. Hundreds of Trinity fans set off but then got stuck on the motorway. By the time most of them got in, we were already 10-0 ahead, soon after 14-0. We'd been 150/1 to win the Grand Final and were now on the way to the final eliminator.

Missed conversions haunted us though, as the Warriors dragged themselves back into it, closing the gap to 14-12 as the game reached its last ten minutes. Adrian Lam dived in from acting-half and it was all over. Losing that match is still one of my biggest disappointments. We should have beaten them and then I'd have backed us to go all the way with the confidence and energy we had. We'd given Wigan a hell of a fright but, ultimately, they had just been too good for us. It was the end of the season and also my time at Belle Vue.

Leaving wasn't straightforward. My career was starting to kick on and I began thinking about winning things and how I could fully establish myself as a Great Britain international. I was still happy at Trinity, after all 2004 had been a turning-point campaign, but I had to determine where I was going next.

I was queueing at the Co-op in Ackworth in early Autumn when my phone rang. It was Jamie Peacock and, while I waited to pay for my loaf, we exchanged pleasantries. He told me how excited he was about me signing for the Bulls. 'We are going to win Super League again next year,' he enthused. 'We can't wait for you to join us.' Nor could I. Bradford had been the biggest and most successful club since the game's switch to summer; three titles, two Challenge Cup wins and two World Club Challenge victories were evidence of that. It had been an open secret that year that I was considering leaving Wakefield. It was now a question of when and where – not if – and that increasingly looked like it was going to be Odsal.

Huddersfield had shown a bit of interest and there was an early approach from St Helens. Trinity offered a deal to stay that would have made me the best paid player at the club but harmed their ability to recruit under the salary cap. Taking the money and staying was tempting, very much so, and I also felt a great deal of loyalty to Shane McNally, but it didn't really give me what I wanted – to be surrounded by international players and win things.

The Bulls were first out of the blocks, then it all got a bit murky. As I was under contract to Wakefield, they'd have to pay a transfer fee for my services and it started to emerge that they couldn't afford it. Instead, they wanted to let me stay at Wakefield, top up my wages, and then take me on a free transfer at the end of the 2005 season. Then they changed their minds and decided they needed me sooner and would offer a player exchange instead of a lump sum.

That's when Shane McNally told me that he had been given the telephone numbers of two Bulls players being touted as part of the deal. When he rang them to discuss the situation and possibility of them joining, both were slightly bemused. It appeared their intended future hadn't been mentioned to them. That threw up a red flag which made me question the whole move. It all began to feel a bit tasteless and, at that point, I remembered something else that JP had said when in the queue at the supermarket: 'I'm not sure what I'll be doing yet.' I didn't think too much of it at the time, but now it very definitely rang alarm bells.

I decided I'd rather stay at Wakefield than cause any upheaval. It was a big call. I had the opportunity to play for the best team in Super League and pick up a pay rise, but it just didn't feel right.

The 2004 campaign had kept me firmly in the frame, however, and when the time came for the new Great Britain head coach, Brian Noble, to choose his international squad, I was delighted to be in it for the new Tri-Nations against New Zealand and Australia.

I felt less awkward than I had the year before, but not much. It helped that there were one or two new guys in the squad, Danny McGuire – who was to become one of my best mates in the game – Stuart Reardon, Ryan Bailey and Sean O'Loughlin. A few days after coming together, we were in Spain again at the same place. But this time, rather than training with the fringe players, I was thrown straight into drills with Jamie Peacock, Adrian Morley and Andy Farrell. I felt quietly confident I would be in the team for the start of the competition and was chosen at loose forward against Australia at the Etihad in Manchester, in front of over 38,000 supporters.

It was relentless and exhausting, the outcome all too familiar. We led early on and were level with three minutes to go, yet lost. I was struck by the performances of Paul Sculthorpe and Farrell. They seemed to carry most of the weight of responsibility for the team in those days. It was no surprise that when cool heads were needed at the end, both were exhausted. Although they were great teammates, I am also sure there was a rivalry playing out between them.

I felt I'd played well and was hopeful I'd done enough to keep my place against the Kiwis the following week. But this was the period when coach Nobby was wrestling with a problem of how to squeeze Paul Sculthorpe, Danny McGuire, Sean Long and Andy Farrell into three positions and he dropped me to the bench.

We won, but the build-up to the next game against Australia was hampered by illness. I was one of a few to catch norovirus, hooked up to a drip for a while, the worst symptom being lack of energy. Unsurprisingly, we started slowly then hit back to lead 18-6 at the break. 'We will not let this one go,' Farrell insisted in the dressing room. We scored next which settled our nerves and held on to win, 24-12, our first triumph in three years against the Kangaroos.

On the bench alongside me that day was Sean O'Loughlin who made a big impression on debut, another reminder that I had no entitlement to a place and so worked even harder in training that week. Already qualified for the final, if we beat New Zealand in Hull we'd finish top of the group. In the middle of the week, I learned that Scully was injured and I was back in the starting thirteen.

Victorious, it was the first time Great Britain had won three in a row since 1993. Reporters were already tipping us to win the final and perhaps we let the idea get into our heads. On the Monday, we went to the International Awards at the Royal Armouries in Leeds. Much to the bemusement of some of the Australian press, most were won by Brits. Andy Farrell was Best Forward of the Year, Nobby was named top coach, Wigan were Club of the Year and the main award, the Golden Boot, also went to Faz. It was hugely provocative and the Aussie press had a field day. It must have played straight into the hands of Wayne Bennett and the rest of his coaching team.

Afterwards we were given a few days off, so I went home for a break. Elland Road was going to be sold out and I couldn't wait. I felt I'd done enough to keep my place, but if the coach needed to squeeze Scully and Faz into the back row and put me on the bench, I'd be content with that. On the Friday afternoon, after we'd returned to our hotel from training, Brian said he was still undecided between me or Sean O'Loughlin for the last substitute place.

I was devastated. Nothing had prepared me for it. The next day, we drove over to the hotel in Bradford we were using as our base prior to the game and I still didn't know whether I was going to play or not. I asked Lockers if he knew. He shook his head, looking as anxious as I was. It was the morning of the biggest game of our careers and we still had no idea if we'd be involved. Eventually, Noble confirmed he'd picked Lockers. His selections had confounded some journalists throughout the series. The disappointment had been unnecessarily drawn out and must have shown. I just wanted to get in my car and drive home. As I watched Lockyer take our defence apart I felt empty and afterwards skipped the reception.

From 2005 onwards, I was a first choice for my country until I decided to step down from international duty in 2013. That 2004 final was the only time I was dropped. I got on perfectly well with Brian and still do, but he wasn't always the best at imparting bad news. In many ways, he was very close to the players, more like one of the lads, a different leadership style to Tony Smith or David Waite.

Having turned my back on Bradford in the autumn, it was then that Leeds showed their hand. Not only did they make it clear the transfer fee wasn't going to be a problem, Headingley was the right place at the right time. I remember going to the 2004 Grand Final in which Leeds overcame Bradford in an epic game. It was a young Rhinos team, winning the title for the first time in decades, and there was a sense that Bradford's dominance of Super League might be coming to an end. Afterwards, Kevin Sinfield was making his way along the terraces through the celebrating crowd to see his family. He saw me and made a beeline my way. Still in his wet and muddy kit, he grabbed my hand and said, 'Gaz, I'll get in touch with you, and we'll have a talk.' Already that was the measure of the man.

The clubs agreed a transfer fee, I just had to confirm I wanted to go but, like every major decision I've had to make, it wasn't quite so simple. Towards the end of that season, I was called to a clandestine meeting at the prestigious Oulton Hall on the edge of Leeds. The men on the other side of the table were keen to keep their approach under wraps.

Although they were league men by upbringing, Joe Lydon and Phil Larder were, at that time, part of the coaching set-up of the England Rugby Union team. Joe had just been appointed as backs coach and, during our meeting, spoke of the success he envisaged for me in union at inside centre. He spoke about Stirling Mortlock playing in that position for the Australian Wallabies. Joe had watched my career and believed that I could emulate Mortlock.

At that time, the RFU were trying to poach a number of players by recruiting them to the national team and then finding a suitable club to join. It was very flattering, but I had never really been a fan of rugby union and didn't know much about it. I left the meeting with a promise that I would think about it but, deep down, I wasn't interested. Leaving Wakefield would be a wrench, leaving the sport unthinkable. Lydon continued to send me DVDs of Mortlock, which I watched with only mild interest. I had barely achieved anything in rugby league and was still only learning about my game. I gave it serious consideration, but the timing wasn't right and it came to nothing. It was a decision about which I have no regrets and one I'm sure my grandad, Tom, would have been pleased I made.

Most of the players at Leeds had been together for a couple of years and many of them were from the city; there was a sense of something special building. Kevin was already the leader. He was only 24 but epitomised everything already good about the club, passionate, determined and absolutely clear about what he expected from everyone. They were all the same – young, driven and like-minded – but the man in whose image the Rhinos were cast was head coach Tony Smith.

On my home debut against St Helens with over 20,000 supporters squeezed into Headingley, we were just ahead in the second half when I took the ball wide on the left. I stepped outside and set off down the touchline. It was a gamble but I was sure there was enough space. I wanted to make an impression, show my speed, but it didn't work. The Saints defenders grabbed me and bundled me into touch in front of a baying South Stand. As the men in the red vee hugged each other, I was fuming at my error, got to my knees and punched the ground in frustration.

Next morning, we were back in for rehab, milling around our Kirkstall training ground. Tony caught my eye and nodded his head in the direction of his office. Apart from the misjudgement, I'd had a decent game, so I wasn't really sure what he wanted to speak to me about. I'd only been a Leeds player for a few months, so didn't know Tony's ways. 'Yesterday, when you got carried into touch,' he said. 'You were disappointed, weren't you? And you punched the floor. You don't need to show that. You just have to get up and carry on with the game.'

At the time I thought it peculiar, but it was part of his philosophy that you show no weakness. If you're exhausted, you don't stand around puffing and blowing. You don't put your hands on your head, you don't even rest them on your hips. You do nothing to tell your opponents that they might have an edge. At half-time, you don't drag yourself off the pitch as individuals, you come together in a huddle and jog meaningfully off as a group, so your tired opponents see you dash past purposefully.

Tony's methods weren't everyone's cup of tea and they took some getting used to. One day, I was on the bike working hard, thinking about how much effort I was putting in and how much fitter it was making me. Tony wandered over. 'Tired, are you?' he asked. 'Yes,' I gasped. 'Okay, but nobody else needs to see it, do they?' he said.

It was all about detail with Tony. We'd spend hours catching the ball. He wanted us to do it in both hands, palms facing outwards in front of us. We'd train for ages, one half of the squad against the other, everyone expected to catch the ball in that way.

When I joined Leeds, my skill set was still fairly underdeveloped. Most of my previous coaches had helped me to progress mentally and emotionally, but Tony took my basic skills to another level. He was the perfect coach for me at that stage, I lapped it up. Nor did his influence end there. Like John Harbin, he had a way of getting inside my head, particularly when it came to club discipline. Before Tony arrived, the Rhinos had been bruised by a couple of incidents where it had let them down. Tony and CEO Gary Hetherington were both determined that the players should not repeat those mistakes.

My first game for Leeds was the World Club Challenge against Canterbury Bulldogs at Elland Road in front of a sell out 37,000 fans and I felt like a fraud. My new teammates had earned the right to be there after winning Super League the year before. I felt like a guest player in a testimonial, even though it was a tremendous experience facing the likes of Sonny Bill Williams, who introduced himself with massive hits on Marcus Bai and Ryan Bailey. It convinced me though that I'd made the right decision to move there from Wakefield. I could compete against the best in the world and, subconsciously, maybe wouldn't mind having a crack at them every week.

I had always known that Leeds was a bigger club but nothing really prepared me for the difference. We trained in Kirkstall, at our own training ground, our base. There was a gym, changing rooms, showers, a video room and a kitchen upstairs, where we went at the start of each day to have our breakfast served. Either side of this complex were two full-sized pitches. One looked every bit as lush and immaculate as our surface at Headingley. I later learned it was exactly the same size to the inch.

At Wakefield, all the staff had seemed to do more than one job. Steve the groundsman was also the kitman. His wife cooked our meals. Owner Ted Richardson's son worked in the club shop. His daughter, Diane, was chief executive. It was a family affair run on a shoestring. At Leeds, there were three physios and another three guys looked after the strength and conditioning. By the time I left Belle Vue, I considered myself one of the fittest and strongest players, but at Leeds the standard went up a notch. Pre-season, we took to the hills of Roundhay Park. Tony would stand at the top and watch us running up and down. I was amazed at how hard those lads trained. Richie Mathers was designated 'head of enthusiasm' and, as he reached the top, he would shout: 'You won't break us, you'll never break us.' Tony would then demand another circuit.

Matt Diskin's philosophy was to go flat out for as long as he could but, before long, he'd be doubled over, throwing up into the bushes and he wouldn't be on his own. Rob Burrow even crashed his car after running the hills one day. He had worked so hard that when he got behind the wheel he couldn't stop his legs from shaking. He ended up wrapping it around a tree.

Ali Lauiti'iti was one of the strongest men I ever encountered and one of the nicest. During weights sessions, he would match me kilo for kilo and then, when I was done, he'd finish too. He'd even grimace a little with the last set and then, when my back was turned, would head back to really challenge himself.

I scored my first try at home to Widnes and got another in the second half. Returning to halfway I heard the South Stand singing my name. It felt great but, not wanting to get ahead of myself, I just trundled back. As the song faded out, I sensed boos. I wasn't sure if I'd heard correctly until Barrie McDermott explained I was supposed to give them a clap. I made sure to remember that next time.

It takes time for your loyalties to change, but by the time we played Wakefield I felt like a proper Leeds player and wanted to put in a performance. I still lived with Steve Snitch, who spent most of the week winding me up. I tried to ignore him putting posters up all over my house and stuffing his Wakefield training kit under my duvet. He had the last laugh too as Trinity put forty on us. I was really upset by that and not just because it was our first defeat of the season. I feared the Wakefield lads would give me a hard time, but they barely acknowledged me, which was even worse.

By the midpoint of the season, we were top of the league, still averaging more than forty points a game and had lost just that single time. My first return to Belle Vue came in June. Ali came off the bench and was unstoppable, scoring an incredible five tries. As the clock ticked down he broke through again and slipped the ball to me to score the final touchdown; it was almost too perfect.

We could not have been in better shape as we reached the business end. By mid-August we were top – albeit just two points ahead of St Helens – and reached the Challenge Cup final against Hull. The last thing we wanted the week before it was a game against Bradford. The Bulls had been quietly re-building after a poor start and shook us up that night. Defeat to them at home was bad enough, but we also lost Danny McGuire and Keith Senior to injuries.

The Challenge Cup has always been magical to me since that trip to Wembley to see Cas win in 1986. Each year, I would sit with my dad on that first Saturday in May and watch the decider as soon as it started on *Grandstand*. The old stadium was being rebuilt, so the final had to go 'on the road' for a while, which is why Tony Smith decided we would treat it like just another game, I suspect. For whatever reason, we chose to wear tracksuits, Tony wanting to keep the lead-up as normal as possible, but I missed dressing up formally and the traditions I'd always seen sides adhere to as a fan.

Keith was still hobbling on Friday morning when we had a walk around the Millennium Stadium in Cardiff. At times like that, you have to trust the judgement of the player. He would have given it great deal of thought before putting his hand up to play. In the event, he made it to half-time and then had to come off. The atmosphere was suffocating. It felt as though the air was being sucked out of me, but the game opened up in the second half and we were 19-12 down.

We'd smashed everyone all season and hadn't come from behind too often. It was an unfamiliar feeling to be chasing a game but, fortunately, we had time on our side. Mark Calderwood scored with a typically mazy run and in the next set we were ahead. But a five-point lead is a precarious one and Paul Cooke's late try left Danny Brough a simple conversion to win the game.

As he crossed the line, Cooke raised his arm to the Hull fans. That wound me up and, as he dived to the floor, without breaking my stride, I trod on his ankle. It was only years later when I found myself doing a Q&A with him that I confessed to what I had done. In the Hull camp, they had talked about it being their destiny. Coach John Kear made a big deal of it in the build-up, and some of our lads played right into his hands and tried to intimidate the Hull boys. I didn't notice it at the time but, later when I had joined Hull, Andy Last told me that they had been wound up by Danny Ward and Ryan Bailey, whooping and hollering in the tunnel before the game. I don't know about that. I don't remember it, although I can't imagine that Danny and Ryan would have been silent either. It's strange what makes you believe you'll win. You can build a narrative to explain what is often just happenstance. It was immensely disappointing to lose, but I just assumed we'd get back to another final soon and put it right. In fact, it took another eleven years for me to do so – and ironically with the black and whites – which only goes to show that you should never take anything for granted.

After Cardiff, the wheels came off. We slipped off the top of the league and finished second. It was a top-five format in those days so we had our first chance of making it to Old Trafford with a visit to Knowsley Road in the Qualifying Semi-Final. After four defeats in five, we weren't favourites, but turned up and got the job done.

I've played in a lot of big games across the world, but nothing has ever compared to running out at Old Trafford in a Super League Grand Final. The atmosphere is the best I've ever experienced. The tunnel isn't particularly wide, so you're very close to the opposition. You walk out from a corner of the pitch, so can see big swathes of the stands as you emerge. There is fire shooting into the air and the noise of fireworks overhead, then the roar of the crowd; you can feel it in your chest. Your mouth goes dry and you have to keep taking deep breaths to slow your heart rate down.

The emotion went up a notch the night before as each of the players, in a quiet meeting after dinner, spoke about what victory would mean to them. The emotions were always most raw among the guys who'd be leaving, in our case Marcus Bai, Chris McKenna, Mark Calderwood, Andrew Dunemann and Barrie McDermott, all moving on to pastures new. For me, it was about wanting to be the best I could possibly be, that drive for constant improvement.

Usually, your body settles down once a game starts, but not in a Grand Final. The pace and pressure never end. After 15 minutes, I looked to the touchline and saw Barrie come on. It was a reassuring sight. I wanted him alongside me, taking some heat off us, but knew exactly what he was going to do next.

Ex-Rhino Adrian Morley had spent the past five years playing in the NRL. He had made a big impression and was considered one of the best forwards in the world. So, when Bradford announced that they were signing him for the last few weeks of the 2005 campaign, it raised a few eyebrows and they stormed through the play-offs.

Just two minutes after coming on, Barrie launched himself at Moz who went down in a heap. That penalty to Bradford made the score 2-0. Just before halftime, Kev landed a penalty goal after Morley took revenge with a flying elbow and it was 8-6 to Bradford at the break. The antics of Moz and Barrie might have looked like they lacked discipline, but they were doing what they thought was the right thing for their team. I've seen plenty of so-called hard men put their ego and pride first. They become tough guy caricatures, but not those two. However, everything we threw at the Bulls was repelled and they held on to win.

I was struck by the wild celebrations of the Bradford players, pure joy, the like of which I had never seen up close. Midway through the year everyone had written them off. A number of stars were leaving, but they managed to come together and into their own and had done it the hard way. They'd also shown everyone else, including my own team, that if you share a common purpose you can achieve anything.

One week after losing the Cup final, the Rhinos announced the signing of Jamie Peacock. It was a huge coup and in that moment signalled the club's intent. We had the playmakers, the finishers and the hard workers. But in signing JP, the Rhinos showed they were strengthening a culture that was already well developed.

Having him around the training ground meant that things which were already good became great. He was forthright with his opinions and was soon a crucial member of the leadership group. Although he was the Great Britain skipper, there was no suggestion he would take the Leeds captaincy. That belonged to Kevin Sinfield. Kev was very calculated and didn't speak too often. JP sometimes clashed with Tony Smith, but only because he cared so much. After he had been there a few months, JP told Tony that he didn't care much for the club doctor, so we got a new one. Same with the kitman, who didn't last long once JP took issue with him. He was willing to explore every avenue to make us the best sporting organisation we could be. All the lads cared about Leeds, with JP – born and bred in the city and a supporter in his youth – it went further than that.

For the 2005 Tri-Nations there were new faces in the camp and no Scully, who was injured, or Faz, who had gone to union. Probably because of the absence of some of those big characters, I felt more assured about my place which made me more relaxed and talkative.

Our first game was at Loftus Road against New Zealand, just a fortnight after the Grand Final. There was no time for a warm-up and we crashed to a heavy defeat. It was an odd experience. There were as many Kiwi supporters in the crowd as Brits and my only real recollection is being hit so hard under the ribs by Nigel Vagana that I couldn't breathe. Chris Brookes was the GB team doctor and is also an experienced practitioner. In the long hours between training sessions I always enjoyed sitting down with him, often while he ate (the largest portions), listening to his anecdotes.

I was a doubt for the game the following week against Australia and didn't make it. We lost in the Wigan rain, which meant we had to win both our last two games to have a chance of making the final.

First up were New Zealand at Huddersfield in a match that will mostly be remembered for the injury to Paul Deacon. Doc Brookes, given his experience, was usually quite unflappable but even he was worried when he saw the extent of the injuries to the back of his mouth. 'Deacs' was rushed to hospital and we were all thankful for the Doc's experience in what was a potentially life-saving moment.

The margin of victory meant that if we could beat Australia by three points we would sneak into the final. If we got up by eight, we would also consign them to the bottom of the group and play the decider against New Zealand. We couldn't have had a better chance. The Aussies lacked Lockyer, Andrew Johns and Nathan Hindmarsh. They also turned up late to the game, had Craig Gower pull up injured in the warm-up game and Trent Barrett sin-binned twice – and yet we still couldn't get one over on them.

That sense of regret was even worse the following week when the Kiwis hammered Australia, 24-0, in the final at Elland Road, the first time they had beaten them in a series or tournament – not including one-off Tests – since 1952.

I was still only 24, fit and strong, yet blissfully unaware of the toll those intense games would take on me in the years ahead.

9

Tasting Success

AS EVER AT LEEDS, THE 2006 season started very early. In fact, it was still 2005. I understand why the club plays on Boxing Day, there are significant financial benefits. But from a player's perspective, when we are supposed to be a summer sport, it makes little sense, as borne out by an injury to one of our new signings. Mark O'Neill arrived with a big reputation having won the NRL with Wests Tigers the year before and immediately fitted in. A proper Aussie bloke, the group really warmed to him.

He bust his shoulder after five minutes on the field, keeping him out until April. When he returned, however, we could see why Tony signed him. By July he was really finding form, but bad luck struck again, this time in training. We had lost the previous weekend and Tony had a bee in his bonnet about us being soft and not running hard enough in attack. 'One group is going to stand in a line, each holding a tackle bag, and the others will run at them as hard as you can. You're going to show me how tough you can be.'

I ended up at the front of the line, Mark holding a bag opposite. I ran as hard as I could. As I hit the bag, he anchored one leg to brace himself and my knee hit him hard on the thigh. I could feel the jolt and he went down like he had been shot. I'd hit his quad muscle and caused a six-inch tear, so that was the end of his time at Leeds. It was such a blow. I was devastated.

'Buckets' might have only played nine games for Leeds, but his contribution to the group was much greater. He and his wife Belinda were great hosts who would regularly invite the lads round to their house for dinner and his impact on me was massive. I learned a lot from how he conducted himself. He loved a good laugh and a beer, but nothing got in the way of football. He was totally professional, and I realised that it was possible to play at the highest level without taking yourself too seriously. Mark was also instrumental during that season in convincing me that I could cut it in the NRL. He didn't just say it in passing, he spoke at length to me about the reasons why I would be successful and how it suited my game. He was a big fan of mine and, naturally, I was drawn to him as a result.

Our only defeat in the first couple few months was at St Helens, but we stuttered in April and May. The biggest disappointment came at home to Hull in Round 14. Not only did we concede forty points, but we also lost Richie Mathers to a season-ending knee injury. Everyone loved Richie's ebullience. Tony actually said to him once, 'Richie, when we score a try, I want you to be the first person to congratulate the try-scorer. I want you to be the one getting the crowd going.' That was Richie. But it was also Tony to a tee; even planning the try-scoring celebrations in detail.

However, Richie would all-too-often be the victim of Tony's wrath as well. Like all good coaches, irrespective of whether we'd won, each week he would pick on different people, get them to look at their errors. But, always, at the end of the analysis, it would boil down to Richie. As fullback and the last line of defence it was always his fault in the end – and he was always 'Richard'.

If there is one game I'd love to play again, it is our 2006 Challenge Cup semi-final at Odsal. Going into it, Huddersfield were eighth in Super League. Nobody gave them a hope of beating us and nor did we. So strongly fancied, the only danger is complacency and once it sets in there is nothing you can do about it. When JP knocked on three times in the first ten minutes, the writing was on the wall. And after that, our season just fizzled out. Before we drifted away at the end of it, Tony Smith planted a thought in our minds. We weren't hungry enough, he said. For some at the club, simply representing Leeds was an achievement in itself.

The only new signings for 2007 were Kylie Leuluai and Brent Webb. Kylie gave us even more power and presence through the middle and the capture of Brent was a masterstroke, linking our halves and outside backs. We now had threats all over the field. Signing people like Brent, and Scott Donald the year before, was only possible because of the loyalty of people like Kev, Danny and Rob. When the history of the 'Golden Generation' is fully written, that should not be overlooked. Those three in particular could have earned much more money elsewhere, probably half as much again, but there was never any discussion as far as I am aware. They cared too much about Leeds and wanted to win things.

Yet after two seasons at Headingley, other than the World Club Challenge winners' medal I picked up in my first game, I hadn't won a thing. I didn't regret my decision, but knew it was time for us to deliver. Early in the season Tony told us all he was being interviewed for the vacant England coaching job. We had no doubt he'd get it, which only hardened our resolve to turn dominance into trophies, not just for ourselves but for him.

These were heady days with ground redevelopment and the new Carnegie Stand opening. We often played in front of 20,000 people. We started well again and, in May, headed off to Wales for a new concept in the sport, Magic Weekend. Every game of the round was staged in Cardiff over two days with three derbies scheduled. Our match with Bradford was the last of the weekend and our supporters were in good voice come kick-off on the Sunday night. It turned out to be one of the most notorious games in Super League history.

We swapped tries at regular intervals and the Bulls led, 38-36, going into the last fifteen minutes. Bradford were furious they'd two tries chalked off and, in truth, referee Steve Ganson had made some erratic decisions throughout, affecting both sides. With less than a minute left, I drove the ball in just inside their half. Knowing we had to keep it alive, I tried to offload but it went to ground and I was gutted. However, Ganson had blown his whistle and awarded us a penalty, claiming that in regathering, the Bulls had been offside. We couldn't believe our luck.

With seconds left, Kev opted to go for goal to try and earn a draw. The Bradford lads were still complaining to the referee and stomping around between their posts in frustration to such an extent that they weren't paying attention to what happened next. Kev's kick looked accurate at first but then fell away to hit the post, bouncing back into play. With the Bulls distracted, Jordan Tansey reacted first to scoop it up and dive over to score. As we all piled onto him, the Bradford players surrounded Ganson screaming for an offside decision, but he just waved them away and awarded the try. While Kev lined up his conversion, the video screen clearly showed Jordan several yards offside. Afterwards, there were ructions with Bradford claiming they wanted the two league points awarded to them.

That was around the time we learned Brian McClennan had been appointed as Tony's replacement, a further reminder that our days together were nearing their end. In the previous two seasons we had wobbled when it mattered most and were determined that would not happen again, the squad healthy, morale high. Our form though was inconsistent, culminating with an unexpected home defeat to Wakefield. We couldn't do anything right, the crowd increasingly on our backs. We left the pitch to the sound of booing from the South Stand, our season in danger of unravelling again.

In the Headingley bar afterwards, the atmosphere was tense, even a little hostile as the players and staff went up to see their families where sponsors and supporters mingle. Tony took the microphone. He spoke about the situation we were in and a need for patience and support. In a short speech that has always stuck with me, he talked of a difference between fans and supporters. A 'fan'– short for fanatic – will love you when you're winning, but turn their backs on you when you're losing. A 'supporter' will be there no matter what.

Attacking is about instinctive flair and creativity; you can coach that. Defence is about attitude which, as a team, you've either got or you haven't. Never was that better exemplified than in the 2007 Qualifying Semi-Final against St Helens at Knowsley Road after we'd finished second to them. Following an opening quarter that saw both sides post a try, it was sixty of the most gruelling minutes I have ever been part of. Of all the games I have ever played in, it would rank in the top ten, even in 10-8 defeat. We were now in elimination territory and what followed was probably our most complete forty minutes of the season. We smashed Wigan, 36-6.

Grand Final week is special. More than anything, it challenges your mental strength. After nine months, you have to be at your very best when, actually, your body is crying out for a rest. The adrenaline carries you through. It starts with the press conferences and media day. Then there's the scramble for tickets for family and friends and the arrival of the kit. On Friday morning, we had our team run at Headingley and then set off, cheered on our way by the supporters.

The journey wasn't a long one and, as usual, we stayed at the Worsley Marriott. It was a good, no-nonsense build-up. After Tony had talked us through our gameplan, it was over to us. There were incredible tales, many of them being deeply personal and emotional, revealing back-stories some didn't know. Most of us were choked up when Kev spoke, and then JP. I started to feel nervous for my speech but ended it with: 'Never take success for granted. You never know when it will disappear.'

Tony also spoke about me when it was his go. 'I want to win for Gaz,' he said. 'And for the other blokes that I've brought to this club. I signed them so they could win trophies. They've worked so hard and deserve this success.' I resolved to do all I could the following day, as much for him in his final game at the helm at Leeds.

As it's a night game you have all day to think about it, which just heightens the sense of importance. The Grand Final at Old Trafford is also a uniquely northern occasion. It usually rains and under lights the atmosphere is raucous. You hear the last few bars of 'Jerusalem', get the nod from the TV floor manager, a few deep breaths, and you start walking. There are no ceremonials, it's straight down to work.

The first half was similar to the semi against St Helens, we led narrowly 8-6 as two exhausted sides looked to drag themselves from the pitch for a much-needed break. But our group, well-trained by Tony, came together in a huddle and ran off the pitch, scooting past our bedraggled opponents. As we reached the dressing room, JP was already saying: 'Did you see them? They're gone. We've got this.'

We'd run off like that for years, but I'd never felt it made much difference until that night at Old Trafford. I genuinely felt we had more energy than them. The second half went like a dream with 25 unanswered points. It ended up a hammering, yet never felt like it.

There was a lot of emotion that night and Tony was at the centre of it. Come the presentation, I shook hands with dignitaries and gave the trophy a kiss. When I joined my mates at the end of the line, they were all admiring their rings and I realised I hadn't even picked mine up, so had to go back around and get it. I was that exhausted.

For the next few days we were on the booze. We all ate together at a restaurant near Headingley and then did the pub crawl known as the 'Otley Run'. It was great to spend time together but a relief that it was all over. It was also the perfect send off for Tony, who deserved it. In four years, he had completely transformed the culture at Leeds and paved the way for the success that followed. I owed him a great deal. I needed his coaching at that time of my career. His relentless attention to detail sharpened my game, improved my skills and my outlook as a player and a man. I wouldn't be the player I had become had I signed for any other club.

Yet to say Tony Smith was obsessed by detail and statistics would be a mistake. He was never really interested in completion rates, always encouraged us to take risks, safe in the knowledge that if they didn't come off we were tough enough to find other ways to win.

The work we did on the training ground, relentlessly finessing those effort-based aspects of the game, would get us out of all sorts of situations. The kick chase and pressure, getting back behind the ball early to help your mate after returning a kick, making a support run to assist them, they were the unglamorous things that Tony really emphasised, and they worked. We played some amazing rugby in 2007, but also showed we could play tough, win the arm wrestle when it mattered – and we showed character. To overcome the disappointments of ending the season so badly in 2005 and 2006, and riding out our mid-season slump that year, was no mean feat.

10

Jacksonville and More Winning

IN PURSUIT OF BECOMING ONE of the top clubs in world rugby, Leeds never left any stone unturned. That's how we came to be flying to Jacksonville, Florida, for a pre-season training camp and game against South Sydney Rabbitohs before the 2008 campaign.

We trained under a warm sun and had the opportunity to take a look at the mind-blowing facilities of the NFL's Jaguars. Rather than a team bus, the club hired a bunch of SUVs to be shared among the squad, five or six to a car. Ian Kirke was nominated driver for my group on the assumption he was the only one trustworthy behind a wheel. We'd meet up after breakfast and drive together to training, but it was afterwards when the independence of having your own car really helped. We could go off as we pleased to see the sights.

Jamie Jones-Buchanan was the driver for his group and we were all travelling together one day in close convoy, when it became clear he was having problems with his vehicle. After a bit of sputtering, it finally came to a halt in the middle of Interstate 95 – Jacksonville's main highway. Not to leave a man behind, several SUVs suddenly pulled over to the side of the road to help him. I don't know what the locals thought of a troop of big blokes pushing a rental car through the streets, horns blaring left, right and centre, until we found safety in the form of a gas station.

We were there to promote the sport, but soon realised we were just the supporting cast to the Souths boys. We spent most of our time hanging around and waiting for them and it was like that all week which, by game day, had really wound us up.

I had another reason to want to perform well. Unbeknown to my teammates, a few weeks before heading to Florida I had signed a contract to play with Wests Tigers for the following season. The upcoming campaign was going to be my last for Leeds and I was also determined to show the Australians what I could do.

The game was at the local university ground and a 12,000 crowd rocked up. Souths' owner Russell Crowe had brought in a couple of mates, golfer Greg Norman – with his girlfriend Chris Evert – basketball star Dennis Rodman and RZA, a rapper from the Wu Tang Clan, to add even more celebrity glamour. Given the way the press had built it up, everyone expected them to win easily, except us. We really ripped into them in the first half; you could sense they hadn't been expecting it. I was smashing everyone and my team-mates were looking at me as if I was a man possessed. We won and it was all smiles at the end. We swapped shirts and had lots of group pictures taken, but I could sense the Aussies' disappointment.

The biggest change at Leeds was the arrival of Brian McClennan as our new head coach. He came with a good reputation, having won the 2005 Tri-Nations series when in charge of New Zealand, and yet it was always going to be a huge ask for anyone to follow Tony Smith. Normally a coach arrives at a club when the previous one has been sacked, the players are ready for a change and keen to embrace new ideas. But here there had been absolutely nothing wrong with how the team had been operating. To Bluey's credit, he realised that and altered very little on arrival. He was even gracious enough at the end of the season to also credit Tony with the success we achieved.

So deeply embedded were Tony's culture and standards that they had become routine. We didn't need him around to continue being successful, the sign of a great leader. That's not to say Brian didn't bring anything. Where Tony was methodical and everything was about performance, Bluey put more of his efforts into motivation. Some of it was a bit gimmicky for me, but there was no denying that he was a good successor.

We made a blistering start to the season, winning our first four games before we came up against Melbourne Storm in my second World Club Challenge game. It was at Elland Road again and over 33,000 turned up on a blustery wet night with crisp packets and all sorts of rubbish blowing across the pitch. There is always talk of whether the Aussies take these matches seriously, but I could never imagine a side coached by Craig Bellamy taking even a game of touch and pass lightly. Once it started, there was no doubt they were up for it.

This was the second time I'd played against NRL opponents in a couple of months and another great opportunity to test myself and put down a few markers for what I knew was to come. It was a tough, attritional game, the only tries coming in the first half, and we owed our success mainly to Kev's kicking. I had my second World Club Challenge winners' medal.

We racked up four significant wins in two weeks and I played centre in all of them. Clinton Toopi was injured and Brian asked if I was okay there. I was still quite agile on my feet and enjoyed the extra space; it was also good fun playing alongside Ryan Hall, one of the sport's characters.

My abiding memory of my time at Leeds was playing St Helens. We faced them nine times and some of those games were among the toughest I ever played in. They were a champion team of star names but also really great competitors with a massive desire to win with the likes of James Graham, Kieron Cunningham, Leon Pryce, Sean Long and James Roby in their ranks. We knew that if we were to claim any silverware, we would have to conquer Saints somewhere along the way.

Defeat to us in 2007 Grand Final had hit them badly and they carried the hangover into the following season, losing five of their first ten. But once they hit their straps, they couldn't stop winning and went unbeaten for 23 league and cup games after that – a record that still stands.

They beat us at Headingley in June to go top of the league and stayed there until the end of the season. A few weeks later, we faced them again, this time in the Challenge Cup semi-final. The trophy had still eluded me and this would be my last chance for a while to get to Wembley and win it. I don't think it played on my mind in the build-up, but it was there during the game. It was a blisteringly hot afternoon, I threw myself into everything, making over fifty tackles and playing the full eighty. Nevertheless, it wasn't quite enough.

A strong finish was needed to get us to Old Trafford and, after winning our last four Super League games of the season, we again finished second. There was a predictability to it all. We went to St Helens in the Qualifying Semi-Final and lost and then, with our season on the line, had one more chance, at home to Wigan, which we won. Lightning struck twice and we were back at Old Trafford to face... St Helens.

In the back of my mind, I knew that after this game I was flying out to Australia and wasn't coming back, so the result would define my time at Leeds. It's easy to forget now that we were rank outsiders. Their winning streak was the talk of rugby league and they had beaten us three times along the way. We didn't fear them, that's for sure, even though they had an added incentive as it would be Daniel Anderson's final game as coach after four highly successful years there. We knew how we'd felt the year before, determined to send Tony off with a win.

We suffered a blow when Brent Webb failed a fitness test on his back. He was in such pain that he couldn't even travel with us, but his replacement was no mug. Shortly after signing for Leeds, I went to watch the academy side. There was this skinny kid playing fullback that day and he was sensational, fast, elusive, and with good skills. I remember thinking he was one of the best kids I'd ever seen. Lee Smith made his first team debut shortly afterwards and was a regular on the wing, centre or fullback during my time at the club. He'd played and scored in the 2007 Grand Final, but 2008 was his best year. Keen to secure his place in the side, he turned in some big performances, none more so than at Old Trafford, his moment.

We went behind early. A few minutes later I wore a big hit from

Willie Talau and knocked on. Then Jonesy got Danny McGuire's knee in his face and needed to be bandaged up; this was going to be every bit as tough as we expected. Then Lee started to come into it.

Twenty minutes left of my Leeds career and a calmness settled over our team. Although the match was still firmly in the balance, we knew exactly what had to be done. We stuck to our gameplan, to kick early and defend for our lives. Kev – as he had been doing all night – stuck the ball high in the air. Caught in the stadium floodlights, it tumbled through the rain and wind towards Francis Meli. The winger couldn't cope with it and the ball ended up in the arms of Danny McGuire, who weaved his way to the line. There were fifteen minutes to go, but we didn't fancy their chances of scoring twice. Probably, neither did they. In the next five minutes, Saints made more errors than they had throughout all of those 23 unbeaten games. Energy drained from them and their body language showed that they were beaten. We'd done it and backed up, the first Leeds team ever to defend their title and the only side to end the season by winning the Grand Final having also won the World Club Challenge at the start. To achieve that level of consistency over eight gruelling months was remarkable.

In the years that followed, under Brian McClennan and then Brian McDermott, the Rhinos would win five more Super League titles, two Challenge Cups and another World Club title, leaving the 'Golden Generation' glittering with medals and awards. It was a remarkable era for the club and for a once-in-an-era group of players and coaches. I grew close to them all with the time we spent together. It was very special, the medals are proof of that, but reflection allows you the luxury of looking fondly beyond them, to the blood, sweat and tears of pre-season, the practical jokes in the changing rooms and the great sense of camaraderie with everyone from the chief executive to those in the back office.

My choice to sign for Leeds was one of the best decisions I made; I know how fortunate I was. My four years there were everything I'd hoped they would be and I had achieved all I'd set out to.

Timing is everything.

11

The Biggest Leap of Faith

LET'S RETURN TO EARLY JANUARY 2008, when on a typically cold but bright Yorkshire morning I was driving from my home in Wetherby to Headingley for a meeting with Gary Hetherington, the chief executive of Leeds Rhinos. Along the way, I picked up my dad. After three successful years, I was about to commit myself to the Rhinos until the end of 2012.

I'd felt a huge sense of relief when Gary called that meeting. For weeks, I had agonised over whether to extend my contract. As happy as I was at Headingley, I was being seriously courted by Wests Tigers. One minute I was determined to stay at the Rhinos, an hour later, I was just as sure I'd be heading across the world. I always take decisions carefully, never rush into anything, but this was ridiculous, weighing up the pros and cons to the point where I was driving myself mad.

As I've said, money wasn't really the issue, the difference between the amounts on offer was negligible, I just needed a reason to choose Leeds. If they were prepared to put a bit more on my contract, then it would probably be enough to tip the decision in their favour. There was a part of me that wanted to stay in my comfort zone and I was glad I'd now have a reason to justify staying at the Rhinos.

We went first to The Taverners – the exclusive member's club in the middle of the North Stand – and Gary got straight to business. He presented a three-year deal, went through the financial terms and tried his best to convince me there was no other club I ought to be considering. Leeds were going to dominate Super League he told me, and he wanted me to be a part of it. It was all very nice except that I had heard it all before. It was precisely the same deal that had been pitched to us earlier, the only difference being that he was now offering me a testimonial if I were to extend again at a later date.

My heart sank. I had been sure I was going to be offered a better deal and that I'd be able to make a decision there and then, but now I was back where I started. Looking back, I can understand Gary's position. Leeds have a defined pay structure and I was already one of the top earners. Increasing his offer would break it and jeopardise negotiations with other players, especially under a salary cap.

And he was confident I'd sign anyway. Nobody really thought I was serious about going to Australia, not even my dad. I was a shy bloke who liked the comfort of familiar surroundings. I didn't want to make my life any more complicated than it needed to be, and I was very well settled. With that in mind, Gary had every reason to think he'd got his man. I didn't tell anyone at the time as we went for something to eat at the café at the back of Headingley, but the offer had made up my mind. I'd be going to west Sydney.

I first became aware of Australian rugby league when my dad's cousins came back from a Great Britain tour in the 1980s. They returned with armfuls of match programmes and team shirts, as well as great stories of the mystical grounds they'd visited. I was never a fan of a particular team but had the colours of Parramatta, St George, Canberra and Brisbane Broncos all hanging up in my wardrobe. The Aussie league seemed like a fantasy one to me back then.

Once I'd started playing, I became aware of their star players and would watch the national side whenever I could, but I still didn't pay a great deal of attention to their domestic competition. In 2002, as a regular for Wakefield, I played alongside Troy Slattery who'd come over. He saw something in me, the first to mention playing down under. But it was Mark O'Neill who really persuaded me to take the notion seriously. He didn't just float it as a vague idea, he went to work on me. 'You could be fantastic over there and you'll love it,' he told me lots of times.

It was how I came to find myself in Noel Cleal's car, driving around the suburbs of Manly. I was in Australia with the Great Britain team for the 2006 Tri-Nations tournament. My agent, David Howes, was also there with his supporters' tour, a group which included my dad and uncle Graham. Since I was still contracted to Leeds we had to be discreet so, on one of my days off, Howesy and my dad slipped away from the tour group and caught the ferry up to Manly, where I met them. Cleal, a Kangaroo who had also played for Hull and did some recruitment work for the Sea Eagles, picked us up, drove us to the training ground, showed us some of the areas where their players lived and finally took us to Brookvale Oval to meet Des Hasler, Manly's head coach.

Up until that point, it had been a very relaxed affair, chatting about possibilities, but once Des started his presentation we realised how serious they were about signing me. It was very slick and Manly was also something of a romantic option. They had a history of signing Englishmen: Phil Lowe, Malcolm Reilly – one of Castleford's finest, Kevin Ward. In fact – as they told me – they'd never won a Grand Final without an Englishman in their team and they wanted me to be the next in that illustrious list.

Like all Aussie clubs, Manly weren't interested in paying transfer fees so I wouldn't be able to join them until 2009, but it didn't deter them. For me, there didn't seem any point in committing myself so early when anything could happen in the meantime, but by the end of 2006 I had started to understand my worth.

During the 2007 season, Leeds came to me with the offer of a four-year extension; the improved terms offering me security until I was 31. It was the kind of situation most players would jump at, but I hesitated. I wasn't interested in playing for anyone else in Super League, so we never even considered that option, but Howesy had been putting the feelers out in Australia again.

Wests Tigers were quick out of the traps. My old mate Mark O'Neill, a legend of Leichardt Oval, had put in a good word for me there, but North Queensland were also interested. Not only did I have to decide whether to leave Headingley but, it seemed, I had options on the other side of the world. After having made three trips down under by then, I was a big fan of Sydney and really fancied living there, so that ruled out the Cowboys in tropical north Queensland.

I still had a year left with Leeds, but wanted everything settled before the new season began. The offers were on the table from the Rhinos, Wests Tigers and Manly and I just had to decide. Almost every day, for hours on end, me, dad and Howesy sat around the dining room table in my house. We structured any decision around three key areas – the football, the lifestyle and the money, always in that order. Lifestyle was likely to be the clincher. Rachael and I are both very close to our families and we knew we would miss them.

Wests Tigers kept in touch throughout the process, talking about where we'd live, helping to find Rachael a job. Tim Sheens would ring me up for a chat, telling me about the club. He even rang my dad and told him how much he was looking forward to having him over to watch me play. I hadn't even signed and I already felt at home with them and so it boiled down to England or Australia.

Throughout this whole period, Rachael more or less had her bags packed. She had spent a year backpacking around Australia before we met and had loved the place. She didn't try to sway my decision, but I wouldn't need to persuade her. It was the same with my dad. Towards the end of his own career, he'd had chance to play amateur rugby in Australia, but it never happened. He didn't want me to miss out on the opportunity.

If I was serious about improving myself – and I was – I had to give the NRL a go. Something was telling me I had more to achieve, more to conquer and more to experience, and it was now or never. I would be 27 next birthday; it was too good an opportunity to miss.

I chose my moment carefully, waiting until Leeds coach Brian McClennan was sitting alone in the café in our Jacksonville hotel. He had only been in the job a few weeks. I sat down opposite him.

'This is going to be my last year. I've signed for Wests Tigers,' I said, somewhat sheepishly.

He was taken aback at first, letting me explain my decision and then he set about persuading me to stay. When he realised it was futile, he was adamant that I needed to tell the lads as soon as possible.

Back from Florida, I had already told Kev and JP simply because, as captain and senior player, I felt it only right they should hear it first. Rachael and I had also spoken to Danny McGuire and his wife, Lauren, to mull over the pros and cons from a lifestyle perspective. Apart from those few, nobody else knew.

It was in the meeting room at Kirkstall just before a video session that I stood up and announced I had something to say. I could feel my bottom lip twitching as I started to share my news. After three years alongside these blokes, I had absolute respect for them. I feared that they would see my departure as a betrayal of what we were building at the club, but I needn't have worried.

12

World Cup Disaster

BEATING AUSTRALIA IN SYDNEY IN 2006 was, without doubt, the highlight of my ten-year, forty-one game international career.

The low point was, and remains, the sobering fact that neither Great Britain nor England have beaten Australia since – the longest period without a victory over the Kangaroos since we first played against them in 1908. There have been twelve successive defeats since 2006 and I played in seven of them, so I think I know something about the disappointment and the frustration.

After our lacklustre showing in the 2005 Tri-Nations, team manager Phil Clarke resigned. 'The international team isn't a priority in this country,' he'd said, 'and the preparation for international games is poor.'

The 2006 Tri-Nations in Australia was the first opportunity for us to see whether the RFL had taken notice of Clarke's words, and there was a lot at stake. It was the first meaningful trip to the Antipodes by a Great Britain side since 1992. Not only was it a big deal for the players, but thousands of supporters were travelling in tow as well. It turned out to be a crazy six weeks.

The governing body had made changes. As well as getting the

squad together for a few midweek training camps, we also played a mid-season fixture against a New Zealand side chosen from players who were plying their trade in Europe. It was a worthy innovation and, although we beat them comfortably, still a decent test.

My season with Leeds had been disappointing. We missed out on the Grand Final and so ended in mid-September, which at least meant that I had a break before the tour began. The main problem that Clarke alluded to, though, had not been addressed. There had been no change to the number of fixtures that we had to play in comparison to our Australian counterparts.

For ten of our squad, who played in the Grand Final for St Helens and Hull, their domestic season ended on the same day as the Tri-Nations Series began. Not only did we arrive disadvantaged, we also had to play five games on successive weekends if we were to win the competition, while our opponents had alternate ones off.

We were just excited at what lay ahead, but were already slightly depleted. Paul Sculthorpe and James Graham were injured and their Saints teammate, Kieron Cunningham, didn't tour for personal reasons. It meant opportunities for Sean O'Loughlin, Gareth Hock, James Roby and Gareth Carvell.

Phil Clarke had also spoken about the value of playing warm-up matches and the governing body had heeded that advice, setting us up with a game against a rugged representative team in Newcastle. Our opponents seemed more intent on knocking our heads off than playing rugby, but it was a useful exercise which sent us into our first game against New Zealand feeling as prepared as we could possibly be. We stayed in Manly for most of the week and only flew into Christchurch two days before the game. It was my first visit to the country, but I barely saw anything of it. We spent most of our time either in our hotel, on the training ground, or travelling in between.

The Kiwis had already been beaten by Australia twice in the competition before we even arrived, so victory would give us a great chance of making the final regardless of how well we did against Australia.

The match exploded early on when Adrian Morley, playing his first game for three months after a suspension in the NRL, flattened

Ruben Wiki. Moz was just trying to put a marker down and win his own battles, but it backfired. The Kiwi pack seemed to grow a couple of inches after that and, even though we fought back in the second half and I scored my first international try, we lost 18-14.

A few days later, the 'Grannygate' story emerged which revolved around whether the New Zealand hooker, Nathan Fien, had been eligible to play or not. In the event, the game was expunged from the record so New Zealand lost the points, but we didn't gain them.

A few years later, I crossed paths with Nathan again. I was playing for Wests Tigers, him for New Zealand Warriors. As I packed down and offered a few words of encouragement to my teammates, he made a crack about me being a Pom and took the mickey out of my Yorkshire accent. Without hesitation, Chris Heighington jumped to my defence. 'Do you even know which country you're from?' he said. That was just one of the many stories that cropped up during that tour. It seemed that every week there was something dominating the build-up to each game.

Disappointed, we flew the next morning to Sydney to prepare to take on the Aussies. Little did we know that all hell was about to break loose once Leon Pryce spoke to the press. It was one of those things that the media always liked the players to do. A 'Tour Diary', promising a few insights into what it is really like to be an international player on the other side of the world. In 2006, the BBC chose Leon and he was anything but boring.

I don't know if the reporter caught him on a bad day. Like all of us, he would have been missing his family. But whatever it was, Leon certainly had a bee in his bonnet. To be fair to him, he only said what most of us felt, that the Aussie press had no respect for us and had given us no chance. Leon also touched on being homesick and that there were times when he would rather be back home in his beloved Bradford. But then he came out with the line he will never be able to forget: 'I'd rather be on Blackpool beach than Bondi.'

The Aussie press went into meltdown. Leon was portrayed as a 'whingeing Pom' and the whole squad were depicted as ungrateful, or worse. Any Australian that had played in England was wheeled out to describe how terrible Blackpool is (whether they'd been there or not) and the negative coverage of our chances went up a level. Suddenly, there were TV cameras following us around everywhere.

When we went out for a meal, the team bus was followed by reporters on mopeds. We had to work as a squad to try to keep Leon out of the limelight, shield him from the paparazzi. Every front and back page had his face on it under headlines ever more vindictive. It wasn't much fun at the time, but in terms of getting us psyched up for a big game played right into our hands, especially coach Brian Noble, who was adept at motivating a team for a one-off game.

Brian took to wearing a 'Kiss Me Quick' T-shirt around the hotel and, when interviewed, had a lot of fun with the press. He would tell them how great Blackpool was, about the miles and miles of golden sands. Earlier, he had also backed Morley after the media went into overdrive following his assault on Wiki. 'Ban him for twenty games,' Nobby told the press. 'No, make it fifty. Ruin his life.' It was probably the best way to respond. It left them with nowhere to go and it allowed us to use the coverage to our advantage and, as if to whip up the expectations on Leon even further, Danny McGuire pulled out of the side with an injury and so Leon was moved up to stand-off, right in the firing line.

There was an electric atmosphere going into that game, my first at the Sydney Football Stadium. It was one of those venues where, as soon as you arrive, you can feel the hostility. Even with thousands of British supporters filling the stands, it was still going to be very partisan. Nobody in there thought we had a chance of winning. We must have failed to get that memo.

On nights such as those, you can feel the atmosphere in your bones. All of your senses are heightened, you know you're about to be part of something special. Everyone was on edge. Unsurprisingly the game exploded in the first few minutes when Stuart Fielden and Willie Mason clashed after a play-the-ball. Expletives were exchanged, no surprise there, but Stuart raised a clenched fist, as he often did, and Mason reacted in typical fashion, flooring Fielden with a right-hander.

Our skipper, Jamie Peacock, was first on the scene and managed to trade blows with Mason for a few seconds before everyone else arrived, piling in. In those circumstances, I was neither a brawler nor a peacemaker. By then, JP and Mason were pulled apart and it was just about done – but the tension had gone up yet another notch.

A few moments later, Mason flattened Sean Long off the ball and there was another set-to. Incredibly, Longy got up and, after a few stitches, went on to play a blinder. Even more unbelievably, Mason got no more than a warning for a blatant act of thuggery, but again that decision only fired us up more.

With twenty minutes left, Lee Gilmour scored a brilliant solo effort and, as time ticked by, we looked like we would hold on. Longy again produced a piece of magic to get us away from our line and into an attacking position. I followed up quickly to help the attack and a few passes later Kirk Yeaman tipped on to his Hull teammate Gareth Raynor, who dived in at the corner. We had done it.

We were shattered that night, but celebrated the following day. After the build-up and abuse we'd been given we felt entitled to really enjoy the victory. There had been a trip planned for the team anyway but, after that incredible night in Sydney, it became a vindication. My abiding memory of the day was of Lee Gilmour being stripped naked on the team bus heading back to Manly. As he tried to find a seat, everyone gave him a whack as he went up and down the gangway. Gilly didn't mind, he didn't have a care in the world. None of us did after beating the Aussies like that in their own backyard.

Inevitably, there was plenty of fall-out in the press after the game. Fielden had a broken nose so wouldn't be able to play the following week, while Mason got a one-match ban for the punch that caused it. We enjoyed the satisfaction of the victory, turned our thoughts to the next game and flew to Wellington where a win would guarantee a place in the final, but we couldn't repeat the performance and everyone who had played so well in Sydney failed to fire.

Longy, who had been instrumental against Australia, wasn't quite at it and we crashed to heavy defeat, 34-4, the only try of the game being my second four-pointer for Great Britain. It wasn't a classic either, Danny McGuire's kick to the corner was going nowhere until Manu Vatuvei dropped it. I reacted quickest to the loose ball and picked it up to score.

The loss was a real back-down-to-earth moment. In the team discussion afterwards, JP put it down to our poor preparation and there was a suggestion that we had over-celebrated. He had a point. The victory in Sydney had been sweet but, of course, we had still not claimed silverware for it. My experience of Australian players is that they are likely to celebrate victory as we had, but the difference is another reason that I believe has stopped us from beating them on a regular basis. We had proved unable to back up with the intensity needed to win tournaments at this level as opposed to one-off games, something the NRL players were used to week in, week out in their domestic competition, which made it second nature.

The hype around Leon really fired us up, but the following week that focus had gone. We were caught out and now we had just one chance left, again against Australia. Victory would knock them out and we would play in the final against New Zealand. It was going to be a crucial week and so, in the team meeting after the game, JP suggested we keep off the beer. Such a suggestion doesn't mean don't touch a drop. It basically implies, if you want to have a drink, do it in moderation. Don't let there be any reason why you can't prepare to your very best.

Like everyone, I had noticed Longy having a few at the airport in Wellington. He looked a bit glazed over but it wasn't unusual and it was his business, despite what JP had said the day before. At that stage, nobody thought too much of it, until he got on the plane. There, Sean became loud and then started singing. Some of the senior players tried their best to calm things down by swapping seats with the other passengers unfortunate enough to be near him. It all got a bit uncomfortable and, by the time we had landed and arrived at our hotel, for whatever reason, Sean had told the coaching staff and a few of his St Helens teammates that he wanted to go home.

Efforts were made to change his mind. We didn't need the media furore that would break out and we also needed him in the team, but it was no use. As the rest of the squad were going through their paces in a recovery session on the beach, Sean was already at Sydney airport on his way back to England. Being away from home for six or seven weeks isn't easy for anyone. Add to that the pressure of performing at the highest level and it's no surprise blokes struggle to cope with it. At the time, Longy's partner was also pregnant and he had just had a nightmare for his country. There are many ways you might try to deal with that pressure and Longy, an emotional guy anyway, chose his. It would be too easy to rush to judgment.

Over the years, I have spoken to lots of older players who toured Australasia long before we had our creature comforts. I recall Keith Hepworth telling me how it took them several days to get there, with six or seven refuelling stops along the way and then, once they finally touched down, they played a game that same afternoon! Johnny Whiteley remembered touring in the 1950s, when the squad would sail to Australia, being away for six months or more. So I do know we have it much easier with our business class flights, shorter tours and constant Skype and FaceTime access to our families.

Even so, it's still not easy. Having been away from home for a month after a gruelling season, Longy, like the rest of us, could not wait to get to the end so we could just go home. His departure did not bring an end to the siege mentality that gripped our camp. Brian Noble, determined not to let the press have their way but also, I suspect, enjoying every minute of it, hung big sheets up at the gates of our training ground to prevent picture-taking. He also enforced a media blackout, banning us from talking to the press.

With Longy gone, Nobby opted to bring in Richard Horne and paired him with Danny McGuire in yet another halfback combination for the final game in Brisbane. It was a hell of a challenge for two youngsters to be up against Darren Lockyer and Johnathan Thurston. They were totally outplayed, unsurprisingly. We were never really in the game, always chasing it.

Late on, Brent Tate was in the clear and racing for our line, but I found the energy to give chase. I nearly had him as well. He wore a soft neck protector, the consequence of an injury earlier in his career. It was tucked into the back of his shirt and came up around the base of his head. As I dived to grab a hold of him, it was all I could get my hands on. I fell to the ground with it in my hands, while he carried on running and dived over. It summed up our performance; we were brave but not good enough.

In 2007, New Zealand were in England for a three-game series, but our 3-0 win was never given the credit it deserved. Some of their star players had pulled out – there was no Sonny-Bill Williams or David Kidwell – but they still brought a team that included Clinton Toopi, Roy Asotasi, Fui Fui Moi Moi and Frank Pritchard. The Baskerville Shield was the first trophy that any of us had won at international level and it was my first medal in a Great Britain shirt.

Our performance in the 2008 World Cup was overshadowed by a rift within the England camp, a demotivated and under-prepared squad. Shortly after the tournament, the RFL surveyed the players for feedback as part of a wider review. It was nothing new, over the years I have done them numerous times for club and country and they rarely provide much insight. Most of the players have moved on emotionally by the time they write the comments and many of them pen such clichés as they feel the coaches want to hear.

There are numerous reasons why England performed so badly in that tournament but the main one is no different to why we always fail at the highest level, namely that our players play too many games.

For most of us involved, and particularly someone like me who tends to keep himself detached from rumour and intrigue, there just wasn't much to say. It wasn't the best of camps I was involved with, nor was it noticeably the worst. For an understanding of what went wrong, you have to go back to Old Trafford and the Grand Finals of 2007 and 2008.

For two years running, St Helens had been the best team in Super League, finishing each season in first place, just ahead of Leeds. Then, following the play-offs, they met us in the Grand Final and on each occasion we beat them. I remember the reaction of the Saints players on the pitch at Old Trafford afterwards in 2008, they were truly devastated. Their dominance throughout the season had counted for nothing and it really hurt them to see us cavorting around the pitch with the trophy.

Although we were friendly enough to one another on the surface, the players were not especially close and had spent two years plotting one another's downfall. Three days after that colossal tussle, Tony Smith announced a 24-man World Cup squad and it was dominated by those two groups; eight players chosen from Leeds and seven from Saints. None of us gave it much thought at the time but, with hindsight, it didn't take a rocket scientist to realise what could go wrong if we weren't careful.

It might have been different if the squad hadn't already been hit by a number of injuries. It would have been a more balanced one if Sean O'Loughlin, Paul Deacon, Terry Newton, Sam Burgess, Jon Clarke or Andy Lynch had been available, as none of them played for those two clubs. Nor did it help that the England coach was Tony.

He was no longer at the helm at Headingley, but had spent years plotting the downfall of St Helens, looking for the weaknesses in their players. Now he had just a few weeks to build them up and integrate them into a coherent squad. His style was not to everyone's taste either. His strengths were not those of John Kear or Brian Noble in terms of engendering a team spirit and a sense of 'we're all in this together'. Tony was subtler than that.

At Leeds, it took him months to create his type of relentless, uncompromising, eye-for-detail culture. It was never going to be easy to do that with England. Nor did he put in place activities to bring the cliques together. In those first few days, I didn't even notice that I was spending most of my free time with my Leeds mates. We got to choose who we roomed with so I shared with Danny McGuire.

Before the competition began, Jamie Peacock spoke to the whole squad about how he felt going into the World Cup, that this mattered more than anything else in his career and he was determined to give it everything he could. He then said he wasn't going to touch any alcohol for the duration and hoped everyone else would join him.

That wasn't going to be a great hardship for most blokes. Nobody wanted to let themselves or their teammates down by being not at their best at training due to having been out late. There would always be down time and because this message of temperance had come from the captain and was, no doubt, endorsed by Tony, we all went along with it – certainly there was no dissent.

Or so I thought.

Coach and captain were both trying to impose a culture that had prevailed at Leeds for the previous few years, but at St Helens they did it differently. They enjoyed a drink together and were given more freedom and responsibility to manage their lifestyles, just as long as it didn't affect their performance. It was part of what made them a successful team and now they were being told that the culture they were used to was going to change. The seeds were sown.

On the face of it, we were still as well prepared as any national team had ever been as we flew out of Manchester. We went business class, stayed in a luxury hotel on the Gold Coast and seemed to have done everything right ahead of our opener with Papua New Guinea.

It was a complicated format which meant that we only had to win one game in order to make the semi-finals. The match was played in Townsville, where there is a large PNG diaspora and a climate more suited to our opponents. We flew up from Brisbane on the Wednesday beforehand, which gave us only two days to acclimatise.

It was the first time I had played at Dairy Farmers' Stadium, a former trotting track ringed by three open-air terraces in the dusty outskirts of the town. Plenty of tour groups had arrived and one included my dad and uncle Graham, but the Brits were still heavily outnumbered. Nowadays most of PNG's national side play together in the Queensland Cup competition, so they have developed strong structures and are well-disciplined. Back then they were still an unknown quantity. We understood, though, that they were fiercely competitive with a style that walked on the edge of the rules. There were rumours that a witch doctor would be meeting us off the plane and as we ran onto the pitch for the warm-up we were berated by a local. 'They're gonna kill yer,' he screamed, over and over again and he wasn't far wrong. In the first few tackles, they were flying at us in gangs from all angles.

It was a very difficult game, and I was partly to blame for their first try. I wasn't often caught napping in defence, but when Rod Griffin surged between me and James Graham, I barely got a hand on him. We struggled throughout the first half, were relieved to be only 16-12 down at the break and lucky not to fall further behind in the second forty, before we gradually crept back into the contest and won, 32-22. We knew that we had underperformed and, afterwards, the press let us have it with both barrels.

Tony tried to put a positive spin on things but the performance had put us under pressure for our next game against Australia. We weren't necessarily expected to win, but a better display was essential as we flew down to Melbourne. While we laboured in Townsville, the Aussies had cruised to victory over New Zealand. There is nothing more ruthless than an Aussie press when their team is on top and we were hammered by their media, day in and day out.

On Thursday, some of our lads had been expected at a press conference to promote the upcoming game, but it was cancelled when the NRL decided instead to hold a media launch for State of Origin. As if that wasn't insulting enough, many of us were then invited to a reception celebrating one hundred years of fixtures between Australia and Great Britain. They showed footage of their great victories with a handful of clips – in black and white – of ours.

But it turned out they weren't far wrong. We started badly, our heads dropped and the last twenty minutes were an embarrassment; 52-4 was England's heaviest-ever defeat. Now it wasn't just the Aussie press that were giving us a hard time, even the usually supportive English journos were as well, and we deserved it.

I have always felt privileged to play in a strong international pack. Even now, we can name one to match it with the Aussies and Kiwis. In the backs it has often been a different matter. When I first started out, we had Kris Radlinski, Gary Connolly, Keith Senior and Iestyn Harris. But, by 2008, the quality and depth weren't there and the Aussies picked off our guys one by one, targeting them and preying on defensive weaknesses, shattering their confidence. The Aussies on the other hand were blessed with speed, power and athleticism in their threequarters; players like Matt Cooper, Mark Gasnier and Greg Inglis. As forwards, we would work incredibly hard to gain position and build a stake in the game, only to see it shattered by defensive lapses out wide or a dropped ball coming out of back-field. It was pretty demoralising.

The following Tuesday, we flew up to Newcastle for our last group game against the Kiwis. With earlier victories, we had both already qualified for the semis, but we desperately needed an injection of confidence. By this stage there was a lot of pressure in the camp and it showed in some of the comments coming out of our group. There was negativity about the choice of Tony Archer as referee again, the Australian who had also been in charge when we were hammered by Australia. Some of our concerns were genuine but it was a bit rich to be complaining about the ref when we had conceded fifty points.

There was a sense of desperation in the build-up when Tony suggested that, instead of standing in front of New Zealand when they performed the Haka, we should form a huddle, which would leave some of our players with their backs to them. I'm not sure what purpose that was intended to serve. I always felt the Haka pumped me up before a game – I still remember watching the Kiwi touring team do it before a midweek game against Castleford as a kid – but we all went along with it. The Kiwis naturally thought we were being disrespectful, to which Tony later replied: 'The Haka is what they do, but this is what we do.'

It might have worked as New Zealand were definitely off the pace in the first quarter and we played our best rugby of the competition although, admittedly, that wasn't saying much. At one stage, we led 24-8, but we found a different way to lose. They scored just before half time and we never did again, utterly outplayed, and ended up losing, 36-24. Our humiliation was complete.

Tony couldn't hide his frustration, focusing his complaints on how the ruck speed was officiated, the slowness of it stymieing James Roby and Rob Burrow who were nimble and fast and whose game depended on it. But, more relevantly, rather than finding another way of utilising these players and our other strengths, we focused on trying to compete in the wrestle, where the big Kiwi forwards were masters. I wasn't sure of the wisdom of that. We couldn't get it right and found ourselves giving away too many penalties.

Despite three poor performances and two successive defeats, we were still in a World Cup semi-final in Brisbane again, against the men from the Shakey Isles. By the time we arrived Tony was not a happy man. He refused to discuss his team selection with the media and banned the cameras from our training camp. An Australian referee was named yet again, which only worsened his mood.

This time we showed proper respect for the Haka and, at half-time, despite having played poorly yet again, it was only 16-10. In the second half, I helped set up the position for a try for JP and was having my best game of the tournament before a bust rib forced me off. There wasn't much else to write home about, beaten 32-22.

It was bitterly disappointing and to underachieve so badly was hard to take. As we sat in the dressing room at Suncorp, Tony started to talk. He was very gracious, thanking everyone, including all the staff, for their hard work in preparing for the competition and saying he didn't expect anyone to go out drinking that night as there was little to celebrate. There was silence for a while, not much mood for discussion nor argument. James Graham was the only one to speak. 'I'll be having a drink tonight,' he said, as heads turned. 'I'm a grown man, it's the end of the competition. I've given everything I could and so I'll be having a few drinks.'

It wasn't phrased as a question and he was not asking permission, he was breaking ranks. Nobody said anything, there was a murmur around the room and we got on with our own business. As much as I had great respect for Tony, I couldn't help but admire Jammer, then only 23, for his honesty.

It is with great regret that I look back on the 2008 World Cup. It was the only one I played in and it ended in bitter disappointment. I spent the whole competition wrapped up thinking about the next game, barely noticing what was going on around the camp, so was unable to do anything about the alleged rift, even if I had spotted it. Mulling it over, I don't think there was one. We were a professional bunch, disciplined and stuck to the rules. Should we have done more things as a group? Would we have been tighter if we'd gone out on the ale together? Who knows, but we missed a trick somewhere.

The best teams I have been involved in have always been those where players know each other well. Once you understand someone better as an individual, as well as their family background, you care about each other more. You want everyone in the group to do well and work that extra bit harder to achieve success. The England squad didn't have that kind of team spirit in 2008. We weren't close enough and that element can easily be overlooked by coaches who get too caught up in tactics and techniques.

Worse, I didn't take in the notion that it *was* a World Cup. I treated it just like any other sequence of games and missed out on so much of the tournament and its celebration of rugby league.

Upon reflection, that tournament was a turning point in my relationship with the England team. My international career still had four years to go, but it would never quite be the same again. It was only once I started playing for Wests Tigers that I realised just how loaded the game was against those who played in Super League and began to resent the burden placed on our players. After 2008, playing for England became something of a chore. It upsets me to say that, but it's true. That season, I played thirty-five games before the World Cup started while those in the southern hemisphere had a quarter fewer. Little wonder we found it so difficult to compete.

It really worries me that some of the current England side will never feel the benefit of having a decent break and proper pre-season in order to recuperate and prepare for their next campaign. They'll often go into end-of-season internationals carrying injuries, playing below their peak. They will then return to their clubs late, missing out on the crucial first few weeks of pre-season training, and will frequently start the following campaign with nothing like the kind of conditioning their Australian counterparts will have received and it becomes a vicious circle. The gulf in preparedness is huge by the time they come to play them again the following autumn and their competition is more intense. It's often like being asked to play the best there is with both hands tied behind your back.

It was all too common to go into camp without three or four of our best players, placing an even greater burden on the remaining senior ones to carry more responsibility. It shouldn't be a difficult decision to protect your greatest assets, to make sure that you get the best out of your product and not drive them into the ground.

While I was always glad to be chosen for my country and my competitive nature would have meant I would be gutted if I was ever left out of the squad, in all honesty by the end of each tournament I'd had enough and couldn't wait for it to end.

13

At Home At Wests Tigers

January 2009
Chiswick, Sydney

I'M SITTING ON THE BALCONY of our apartment, overlooking the Parramatta River. The sun is up. Even at eight in the morning the temperature is in the mid-twenties. I think of my family, at home in front of the telly, heating on, a bit worried about the state of the roads as the ice thickens. I briefly wonder about Danny and Kev, JP and the rest of the lads at Leeds, shivering at training, if they had managed to get out onto the ground at all.

I have another sip of coffee and watch the rowers training out on the river in front of me, slipping past the palm trees bordering its still waters. They will be heading back into the Rowing Club, a lovely place I might take Rachael to, for a bite to eat, after my own training. It'll be a nice walk along the river as the sun sets. I jump in my new Jeep. It's not far, ten minutes if I don't hit traffic on the Great North Road, Kings of Leon on the stereo – I think I might enjoy it here.

We first set eyes on our new home – a two-bedroom apartment about five miles west of Sydney – on my day off from England duty during the World Cup. Mark O'Neill's wife Belinda picked us up and gave us a tour of the neighbourhood. As promised, Wayne McDonnell and the rest of the Wests Tigers backroom staff had done a terrific job for us. From announcing my signing a year before they stayed in touch and had delivered with our accommodation. The apartment was on a complex with its own outdoor swimming pool, tennis court and gym. But it was only when we stepped outside onto the balcony that we realised just how different life was going to be.

World Cup duties had ended in Brisbane so, before my parents headed home, Rachael and I met up with them and some friends and had a bit of a holiday on the coast. Gradually, everyone left until it was just us two in our new home thinking, 'What have we done?'

It was December. We had time on our hands, so took off to see some of the country. Rachael organised the itinerary and we went up the coast, to Port Macquarie, then Coffs Harbour and Byron Bay. From there, we drove into Queensland and woke up on Christmas morning in Sanctuary Cove, on the Gold Coast. After swapping presents, we went down to the hotel's man-made beach and then had Christmas dinner in shorts and T-shirts. A great experience but despite the beauty and the luxury, on balance we would have rather been at home in England for more traditional festivities.

Reality TV isn't something we watch in England, but it helped us to learn more about Australia and those who live there. We loved *Wanted Down Under*, which followed the lives of couples emigrating from England. We could empathise with the young people wrestling with a decision that would turn their lives upside down.

In February, the Tigers held a pre-season launch party at Dedes Grill, just around the bay from our apartment. This was a members' only club, not of the working-class type I used to go to with my dad. We took our seats at tables groaning with seafood of every kind. Instead of knives and forks we got pliers and pincers, hadn't a clue what to do. Robbie Farah was on our table and thoroughly enjoyed himself, showing us how to crack open a crab and peel a prawn.

The Aussie season starts later than in England, so my pre-season was longer than I had been used to and we began training in mid-summer, another significant difference. It was shorts and singlets rather than skins and beanie hats, swimming outdoors rather than stuck inside a gym all day. It was one of the best preparations I had, I'd never been in better shape, but it didn't take long on the training ground for me to realise that rugby league blokes are essentially the same wherever you go in the world. The day before my first session, my phone rang. It was Liam Fulton, one of my new teammates.

'Hi Gaz,' he said. 'The lads are really looking forward to seeing you tomorrow. It's going to be great having you at the club.'

'That's really nice, Liam,' I replied. 'I'm looking forward to meeting you all, too.'

'Yeah, mate, we're excited to have a Brit in the team. Some of the lads have been talking, it'd be nice to see your England shirt. Would you come in to training with it tomorrow, so we can maybe get a photo of you and some of our other internationals?'

I dug out one of my England shirts left over from the recent tour and stuck it in my training bag. As soon as I sat down to get changed, Liam saw it in my bag and just started laughing. It was the first time we met and I knew straight away I was going to enjoy his company.

I was well aware of the pressure on me to succeed. If I flopped, it would reflect badly on Super League and the English game. At first, I felt like the new kid at school, desperate to fit in. I had no ambitions beyond wanting to become part of the team and be worthy of a place in the starting line-up. I'd been given a taste of what that might be like the previous year when Leeds played Melbourne in the World Club Challenge. 'Ellis, you'll never make it in the NRL,' their winger, Anthony Quinn, said as a tackle broke up. 'You're going to be a flop.'

'Thanks for that, mate,' I replied, 'but, remind me who you are again?' I was pleased with that one.

I'd done a bit of homework on my teammates. I knew quite a bit about Benji Marshall and Robbie Farah, but most of the others were new to me. Dene Halatau became one of my first mates at the club, a veteran of the 2005 premiership team. He and his wife, Rochelle, lived in the same complex as us and we started travelling to training together and struck up a good friendship with them both.

Chris Heighington was another we are still close to. It helped that he is of English heritage as one of the first issues I faced was making myself understood. I took my West Yorkshire accent over there and didn't expect to have any problems but, in those first few weeks of training at Concord Oval, it became a frequent source of confusion.

Early on, every day was an adventure. We weren't far from the centre of Sydney, but we rarely drove anywhere. We'd get the ferry. Chiswick Wharf was only a ten-minute walk. From there, it was just half an hour into the heart of Sydney. With a full day free, we'd go to the beach. Our favourite was Shark Bay, in Nielsen Park to the east. It was quiet and a bit secluded. Most of my new mates were quietly amused by what we were up to. One weekend the Tigers had a bye, so Rachael and I flew to Tasmania, determined to see as much as possible. We really liked it there. It was a bit like England, cooler and very green, but no one could understand why we'd want to visit.

Training began at nine with a weights session. The gym at Concord Oval wasn't as up to date as I'd been used to at Leeds, but it was more than adequate. In the early part of pre-season if we were running we'd use a public park next door. Concord was comfortable, nothing spectacular, but it soon felt like home.

Because of the training schedule, we found ourselves with an extended break in the middle of the day. We weren't given any food at the training ground so most of the lads would head off for lunch to Rizzo's, an Italian café in the Five Dock area. We would grab some pasta and a couple of coffees but, more than anything, it was a good place to hang out. Once you've had Benji Marshall, Beau Ryan and Liam Fulton take the mickey out of you for a week or so, you start to feel like one of the lads.

We began to socialise on an evening too. This wasn't the heavy drinking culture I'd known when starting out at Wakefield though, far from it. We'd go out for a meal, sometimes with wives and girlfriends, but there would also be a boys' night most weeks.

Before Adrian Morley left at the end of international duty, he introduced me to a bloke named Charlie, or 'Bubba' as he was more commonly known, who soon became a great mate. Charlie was from a big Italian family and every Wednesday night, without fail, they would get together for spaghetti. About once a month, along with a few other Tigers boys and occasionally the Burgess brothers, we'd go along and join in, made to feel incredibly welcome.

I've always taken a bit of interest in the clothes I wear. I wouldn't say I'm a dedicated follower of fashion but, if ever I go out, I'll give some thought to how I look and always dress appropriately for the occasion. The first time we went out with the Tigers players and their partners I wore a smart pair of shorts, trainers and matching short-sleeved shirt. Arriving at the restaurant, all the other blokes rocked up in what I soon realised was the obligatory outfit for a professional football player in Australia – vest, casual shorts (Robbie Farah wore the same ones for all four years I was there) and thongs (flip-flops). We arrived early and as each of them turned up my heart sank.

I don't know who first used the term 'brothers forever', probably Benji or Beau Ryan. It began to be mentioned in press conferences, a phrase that got used around the place, and over that first season I sensed something very special building among the group.

To begin with, I felt responsible for making sure that Rachael was happy and had things to do. She didn't know anyone. It was tough for her to make friends, but thankfully – and with help again from Wests Tigers – she managed to secure herself a job at a children's nursery in Henley, across the river. We got her a car and immediately she had independence, which was great for both of us. Later, after Isaac was born, Rachael joined a toddler group and met lots of other new mums. Soon we had friends outside of rugby league, including a lovely English couple.

Wests Tigers is a joint-venture club formed after the 'Super League war' of the late-1990s, when Balmain Tigers and Wests Magpies came together. The two clubs are based over an hour apart, which I found a bit strange, and it was also odd to see Balmain shirts dominating the hill at Leichhardt Oval, while Wests Tigers shirts could be seen all over the stands at Campbelltown, our playing bases.

It was still a bit raw for some and probably helped me that I wasn't affiliated with either club. However, over time I tended to have more contact with the Balmain side as I became closer to Dave Trodden, a die-hard who was the chair of the Tigers when I signed.

I also preferred to play at Leichardt, Balmain's spiritual home, a genuine rugby league ground – a little like Castleford or Wakefield, except that it also had a hill. The Oval held about 20,000 and when full on a Sunday afternoon, as it often was towards the end of the 2010 season, there was no place like it.

But for now, as the 2009 season drew closer, media interest in me intensified and I've never been particularly comfortable in the public eye. After a few months in Sydney, I started to get recognised. *The Footy Show* was very popular on television, catapulting those who regularly appeared on it to a whole new level of celebrity. I opted out, but there were other parts of the media you couldn't ignore. Even pre and post-match interviews were different to what I was used to.

At a press conference in the lead-up to a game, there'd be twenty microphones in your face and because of the number of media outlets and the competition for stories, each journalist would probe a bit more, trying to unearth a scoop. Their relentless scrutiny only served to raise your game in the knowledge that mistakes or poor performances will be picked over endlessly. When I first arrived, the club helped me to keep a fairly low profile, but once I'd settled in I had to do my media duties like everyone else. Whenever I saw my name on media manager Wayne Cousins's list, my heart sank a little.

I was called upon to play in all three pre-season trials (friendlies, as we'd call them). The first – against South Sydney – was billed as the 'Return to Redfern', the first game played by them at their former home since being renovated, right in the heart of their traditional community. The match was sold out, 5,000 squeezed into the ground in late summer, temperature in the high-thirties. I struggled with it and, although we won, was far from happy with my performance.

A couple of weeks later, I faced Sydney Roosters at the Sydney Football Stadium. After which, we went down to Shellharbour for run out against a local team on the coast. I had grown used to the heat by then and, with three games under my belt, felt ready to go.

The week before my NRL debut, dad flew out. This was a huge occasion for him, having played such a massive part in my career. David Howes came too, as did uncle Graham, my cousin Richard and nine-year-old nephew Jack. I'm not sure how they all squeezed into our two-bed apartment, but we managed somehow.

It was a warm late-summer Monday night at Campbelltown and what the stadium lacked in charm, it more than made up for in noise, close to full. I don't know if it was intentional, but the kick-off came straight to me, landing just short and bobbling several times. It could have been a disastrous start, but I scooped the ball up smoothly, picked out my line and drove into the advancing Canberra defence.

I came up with a few eye-catching moments, including a couple of big hits on the Raiders' wingers, and I might have scored but for a last-gasp tackle. It was a steady debut, nothing amazing, but I had played my part in a win and was relieved and pleased. They even gave me the Man of the Match award, which was a nice start.

Post-match ceremonies were conducted outside, on the terrace. From the darkness surrounding the stadium, unfamiliar smells and sounds drifted in. It felt intoxicating, like the start of the greatest adventure in the world.

A week later, we flew up to play North Queensland in Townsville. It was a three-hour flight and I was still in the same country! That was another exciting aspect of playing in the NRL. We lost against the Cowboys, but I was pleased to have played for eighty minutes in humidity the likes of which I had never encountered. After a few games, I actually enjoyed it and revelled in the punishing conditions.

All was going well and then I came up against Willie Mason at the SFS. Inevitably, he chose me to sledge and the comments were picked up by the TV microphone and made the press in the coming days. After the game, I was walking away from the stadium with my dad when we saw him heading in our direction. Bracing myself for another round of abuse, he couldn't have been nicer. 'Great to see you, mate,' he said, as he shook my hand. 'It's good to have you here. Best of luck for the season.' Rugby league in a nutshell.

Every week was a new experience. In May, we played South Sydney in the heritage round at the Sydney Cricket Ground. It was a privilege to be at the SCG. The changing rooms were old and run down, but history was written on every wall. From just where I was sitting, I could see the names of dozens of famous cricketers that had, over the years, scratched their initials or signatures, the most notable of which was Don Bradman. Instead of cleaning them off, they had covered them with Perspex and put a frame around them, adding to the history of the place. A few weeks later, we flew across the Tasman Sea for my first visit to Auckland and a game against New Zealand Warriors.

Rachael and I also settled into new routines, very different to home and unique to our surroundings. We loved the Aussie version of *Masterchef* and reality TV show *The Block*, in which couples were tasked with renovating houses. Various family members came to visit and we enjoyed showing the sights. I lost count of the number of times we went to Taronga Zoo. My youngest sister Rachel loved it so much that she came back and lived with us for a year.

What came as a real surprise was driving to games. At Leeds and Wakefield, the team would travel together. Even if we were playing just a few miles up the road, we would always meet up at our home ground, board the team bus and arrive as a group. When we were playing in Sydney, we all got there under our own steam, arrived separately and drive home alone as well. It was just one of those quaint idiosyncrasies that I loved about the Australian game.

Another quirk at Wests Tigers was that we had to wash our own shorts and socks. At Leeds, we not only had our playing kit washed but our training gear as well. We would throw all it into a wheelie bin and, when we arrived next morning, it would have been cleaned and laid out for us. After my first game at Campbelltown, I did the same only to have our kitman, Vince, throw the shorts and socks back in my direction. Over time, I also developed my own little fan club. The 'Gaz Ellis Army' were a bunch of supporters who took to wearing camouflage versions of the Tigers' kit.

After four years at Leeds, I wasn't used to getting beaten often but the NRL was different. We came up against quality teams every week who, all too often, were just too good for us. By Round 16, we'd only won five games and sat next to bottom. This was a competition where small margins were so important. If you were slightly off-key even against the bottom team, or missed a couple of chances, you'd get beaten. In England, we say things like 'we played badly but won.' In Australia, if you play badly you lose.

With Benji Marshall and Robbie Farah in the side, we became renowned for flamboyancy but also infamous for inconsistency. I saw my role as a stabiliser whose performances didn't trough and peak. I set myself the goal of doing the job I was asked to do as best I could and began to become more valuable to the team. Tim Sheens kept telling us that a few wins would turn our season around and he was right. We strung together six on the bounce and suddenly were fifth. In typical Tigers fashion, having dragged ourselves back into the play-off positions, we lost our next two games and missed the cut. Our season was over by early September.

A year earlier, my experience of 'Mad Monday' had taken place in the student pubs of Headingley. That was in October and it rained. At the end of my first season in the NRL, we flew to Cairns! 'Mad Monday' was a big thing in Australia, as it is England, except there the antics of the players are scrutinised far more and they are often followed around by reporters. Eventually, the clubs began to take control. One year, Wests Tigers hired a boat for us to cruise Sydney harbour and the Parramatta River in. It was loaded with alcohol and food and off we went, away from prying eyes. But there was still plenty of mischief to be had. A few hours into the party, Chris Heighington decided it was time for a swim and jumped in. When he re-surfaced, the boat was some distance away and he had to be rescued by a small fishing vessel.

The early end had one upside in that we could go home. We were missing England, keen to see our families. I also managed to catch the end of the Super League season and Leeds making their way to and winning their third successive Grand Final. I also furthered my international career with a decent Four Nations campaign.

But Rachael, by now, was thirty-two weeks pregnant and we had to get back to Australia. We just managed to squeeze in one final excursion on our return and flew up to Airlie Beach to take a boat trip around the Whitsunday Islands. And it was there, while staying on Hamilton Island, that I proposed to her.

I asked the club if they might be able to find somewhere a little bigger for us to live in and they agreed. Not only did they secure a larger apartment but – while we were in the Whitsundays – they also moved our furniture, clothes, everything, into our new place. We were hugely grateful. It was in the same complex but on a higher floor, on two-storeys, with a wrap-around balcony on the front and the back that looked up and down the river. It was just amazing.

On Christmas Day, we were at home looking forward to a quiet relaxing day. After dinner, we planned a walk around the bay in Drummoyne in the evening sunshine, until the labour pains started and we found ourselves on our way to Sydney hospital. In the event, Isaac wasn't ready to arrive. We had to wait a bit longer to be parents.

'ONLY THE TIGERS COULD CONJURE THIS!' the commentator told Fox viewers, just after I scored my first try for the club. Having trailed 20-4 early in the second half of the 2010 season opener with Manly we had seemed to be destined for defeat, but came up with a miraculous comeback that culminated in Robbie Farah's toe-poke towards the tryline in the 75th minute. I raced onto it, just managed to take it out of the opposing fullback's hands and touched down.

We won four of the first five but then lost the next four, including getting hammered by 50 points by Souths, which was embarrassing.

Something had to change or our season was going to drift away from us again. Our next game was just five days later, in Newcastle. We travelled up the day before and spent a bit of extra time together, talking about what we needed to do in the coming weeks. By kick-off, the heavens had opened, but we slowly got the better of the conditions and ran out winners. I went well. It was an important win for us, showing we were capable of grinding out victories when it mattered. It also nudged us back into the top eight, where we would stay for the rest of the campaign.

A few weeks later, I asked if I could go to England for the mid-season international against France, in Leigh. We had a bye weekend so I wouldn't miss any games and it was our first chance to take Isaac – who had by now arrived – to meet his family. Wests Tigers weren't too happy but figured that if it was good for me and Rachael then it would be better for them in the long run. Rachael stayed on a little longer; it was always important to us during our time in Australia to maintain contact with our network of friends and family back home. It helped keep us grounded.

After beating Brisbane at Suncorp Stadium in Round 17, we were up to third. But during the game I aggravated a groin problem that had been niggling me for a few weeks. It was a chronic injury called osteitis pubis, inflammation of the pubic bone, and it got worse over time. At the beginning of a training session, it would feel like my groin was tearing, incredibly painful. Once I got warmed up, though, it wasn't too bad and I'd played through. Now it needed rest.

Our revival was based around the talents of Benji Marshall and Robbie Farah in the spine of the side; they were real thinkers about the game. I would often look up from training to find them both in a huddle with Tim Sheens, deep in conversation. Benji, in particular, was a phenomenon. When people saw him stepping off both feet and flicking passes out the back of his hand, they thought it was off-the-cuff, but he used to practice that all the time. I saw it daily in training. He'd play in touch rugby competitions with mates in order to develop his ball-handling skills even more. I'd been apprehensive about Benji when I signed. He was easily the most famous player at the club and I wondered if he might be a bit 'big time', but he turned out to be the exact opposite.

Although those two did most of the talking, I was beginning to find my voice within the team, taking more of a leadership role and speaking up in meetings. It certainly helped that the Tigers were one of the closest squads I had ever been a part of. Some of the players had been around the club since their mid-teens. Match days became family get-togethers and, even when the side were on the road, the families would often meet up to watch the game together on TV. There were barbecues, birthday parties and every Australia Day a Harbour cruise, with everyone invited.

Chris Lawrence was only young when I met him, but even at 21 he was really switched on, a smart guy with a keen entrepreneurial brain. He'd already set up a business to prepare for life after rugby. Mark Flanagan joined Wests Tigers in 2010 and it didn't take him long to settle in. It was great for me to have another Englishman in the team who was making the same adjustment I had twelve months earlier. I enjoyed settling him in. 'Flash' also knew the Burgess lads from their time at Bradford, so we all met up together occasionally.

Beau Ryan was a character. Superstitious to the point of being OCD, he would do the sign of the cross whenever a plane flew over Leichardt. He reckons his superstitious nature comes from when he played cricket as a young man. Facing a fast, intimidating bowler, he tapped his bat with his glove and promptly hit the ball for four. Next ball, he tapped his bat twice and smashed it to the boundary again. For years, Beau had been a regular on *The Footy Show* and nowadays he is seldom off the telly down under.

I came back from injury at the end of July and helped the team to win four of our last six games to make third spot going into the play-offs. I was excited. This was what I had come here for. However, I had no idea that, ahead of us, were three weeks of the very highest drama and controversy. And it began with a game that still ranks as one of the greatest of all time.

14

Play-Off Heartbreak

IT WAS THE ROOSTERS AT the Sydney Football Stadium; Wests Tigers' first tilt at post-season football since winning the competition in 2005. We'd added some steel to our performances – criticised as lacking that previously. Dad came to Australia for a month in case we reached the Grand Final and got himself papped, his photo splashed on newspaper front pages in the build-up.

In twenty-odd years as a professional rugby league player, I never once scored a hat-trick. But I'm sure I must be the only one to have crossed the line three times in the first ten minutes of an NRL play-off game – only to have all of them disallowed.

The second, held up, and third when a scuffle instigated by Benji preceded grounding a loose ball were fair enough, however I blamed myself for the first. I was put into a gap wide on the left and just about to put the ball down when Todd Carney managed to get a hand to it in the tackle. It bounced free and over the dead ball line.

I was gutted, my mind racing, and that was without knowing dad had placed a bet on me to be the first scorer at considerable odds. In the minutes that followed, I let my frustration get the better of me and caught Carney with a high shot. The penalty conceded was in kicking range and they were 2-0 up. We responded, though, and were 15-2 ahead and in control with 20 minutes remaining.

Defeat for the Roosters meant elimination, so they had no choice but to change how they were playing. They started taking risks and suddenly became a different proposition and much harder to defend against. In Carney, they had the Dally M Medal holder, the best in the competition, and he created two tries to bring it back to a point.

We were hanging on desperately and I was absolutely knackered. Normally, facing exhaustion in a game, I can find a few seconds to catch my breath, take stock and carry on. However, the Roosters came down my line three times in succession. I'd put in some huge hits and was gassed. A potential liability, I got a signal to the bench and was taken off. Benji got injured and was withdrawn as well, hastening the most bizarre final minute of any game I played in.

Roosters were building an attack just inside our half. Desperate to shut down the drop-goal chance, Simon Dwyer smashed Jared Waerea-Hargreaves, who spilled the ball. As we began to celebrate regaining possession, the referee judged a knock-on and scrum with our head and ball. Technically, the ref ought to have played on with us in possession, but all we needed to do was run down the final thirty seconds of the game.

Inexplicably, we knocked on at the base of the scrum as Roosters' pack put a push on. They kept the ball around the middle of the field looking for a position to take a drop-goal to level, while our lads swarmed forward trying to shut down their options.

With two seconds left, from forty metres out, ten in from touch, Braith Anasta launched the ball goalwards and I saw his jubilant reaction – golden-point extra-time loomed. I wish I'd stayed on the field. I'd got my breath back and, although my back was killing me, felt fit enough to return. But Tim Sheens had few interchange options left. There was nothing I could do except watch. After five minutes, the sides swapped ends. There'd been half a dozen drop-goal attempts, none of them close. Ten minutes of extra-time went by, more attempts, each one more desperate than the last. This was the first golden-point extra-time in a finals game and, although it was dramatic for spectators, it was torture for the players.

After fifteen minutes of extra-time, the pace of the game slowed dramatically as both sides began to play safe, hoping their opponents would make the error. With the clock ticking past 99 minutes, Liam Fulton's pass wide to the left was intercepted by Rooster Shaun Kenny-Dowall and he crossed in the corner from 60 metres out. I had never experienced anything quite like it. It was only the first round of the play-offs, but it had the atmosphere of a Grand Final.

There is a health club attached to the Sydney Football Stadium and our plan had been to jump into their outdoor pool after the game to warm down. But that would have meant walking past some of our supporters and nobody fancied it after such a gut-wrenching loss. How could we face them after we had blown a lead like that? Which was when Todd Payten spoke up. He kicked everyone out of the dressing room except the seventeen that had just finished playing and shut the door. Then he told us to stop whining and feeling sorry for ourselves. He wasn't the coach or even the captain, but he was the senior guy in our team and very well respected. We all listened to him as he told us to walk out of the dressing room with our heads held high and – most importantly – to do it together.

By then, my back problem had become serious. It had plagued me for weeks and I'd been resorting to painkillers to get me on the pitch. There was no way I was going to miss this part of the season, though, so was prepared to do whatever it took. There's a price to be paid for being a professional sportsperson, especially when you play with injuries. Pain is a natural sensation, warning the body to stop doing whatever it is that's causing it. Everyone plays with injuries and knows that, doing so, you are essentially borrowing against your future health and mobility. My back hasn't been the same since that play-off series and probably never will be.

We were still in the race by virtue of finishing in the top four, so to speed up recovery Steve Folkes, our head trainer, set up our own miniature hyperbaric chamber. It looked more like a body bag. I didn't train that week, it was all about recovery. By midweek, I could barely move, rest the only option. I laid on a sofa hoping for the best.

With a strange system in the play-offs, we were sent to seventh-placed Canberra in an elimination game, with demand for tickets such that it created a ground record attendance. In the event, most of our lads were fit. Benji was back, I was able to make it and even Chris Lawrence, who had broken his jaw just three weeks earlier, returned to the side. The speculation over our injuries had reached hysterical levels in the press and, when we all turned up on game day, we were accused of playing mind-games. I'd have laughed but it might have hurt my back.

That game in the capital epitomised the Tigers, some brilliant attacking play but with awful lapses in defence. I didn't speak up much in team meetings, however when I did it was often about our defence and in order to make myself accountable. I would tell the group what I intended to do so that I had no choice but to go out and do it. Hopefully, they might follow me. We spent hours working on defence but even then a session on it could turn into an attacking drill if Benji, Robbie or Tim had an idea. It was just how they were.

Leading narrowly at half-time and having scored a try, I staggered back to the sheds. I found my normal seat next to Chris Heighington and sat there, head in hands, towel draped over me. Painkillers made me drowsy and so, to counteract that, I'd also taken caffeine tablets. I felt quite spaced out, like my lower back might go at any moment. Tim Sheens was saying something and so were the other lads, but I was in a world of my own. A few more minutes rest, no movement, let the pain go down a bit and then I'll be okay, I thought.

Afterwards, some lads told me I fell asleep, a combination of the drugs taking effect and my body responding to the pain. They gave me a nudge and sent me back out. Once I got going, I was fine. For the second week running we were in control, but they managed to score to make it 26-24. With just three minutes to go Jarrod Crocker had an easy looking penalty shot to level. We had seemingly thrown away a lead for the second week running. As I prepared myself for extra-time, I was mindful of the toll that game six days before was bound to have on our energy levels. I couldn't believe it when he missed; the rugby league gods seemed to be smiling on us this time.

Victory over Canberra had saved our season and we were now just one game from the Grand Final. In front of us we were Wayne Bennett's St George-Illawarra Dragons, the best in the competition

Above: With Rachael, the kids and the Challenge Cup at Hull Guildhall.

Left: Family club – the lads share the pitch at the KCOM with their kids.

Right: Inside the Wembley dressing room in 2017.

Below: A picture taken for a *Sunday Times* interview.

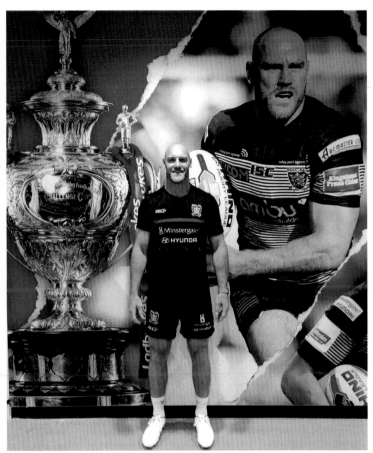

Left:
Meeting
myself again
at Wembley
in 2017.

Below:
We were
much more
confident
that time,
beating
Wigan in
the decider.

Above: Danny McGuire is my best pal and so it was fitting that I played my last game with him – or so I thought! *Below*: After retirement, I threw myself into new challenges including the Rugby League Cares 'Ride to Wembley' in 2019.

Above: St Helens win the Grand Final at an empty KC Stadium in 2020. I walked the trophy out!

Above: On retiring, I threw myself into lots of challenges. Here I am in 2018 on the starting line for the Great North Run in Newcastle.

Right: Raising funds for 'Life For a Kid' with Andy Lynch, Adrian Morley and the great Rob Burrow. The game has made me lasting friendships.

Left: Proud moment – Moz, Paul Wellens, Jamie Peacock and myself receive our Great Britain heritage numbers.

Above: Happy days with Jamie and Rob as we brave the Skydeck in Melbourne in 2018.

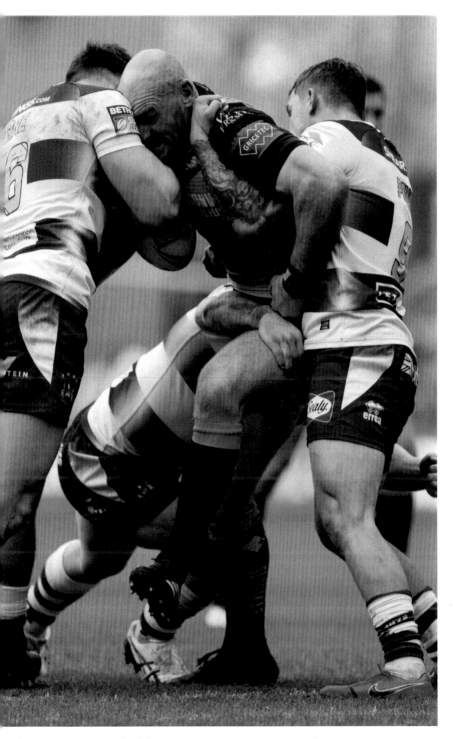

Above: Making my comeback from retirement against Wigan in February 2019

POSITIVES

ENERGETIC, PUSHING
ON PLAYS
STRONG CARRIES,
THREATENING IN ATTACK
EARLY CARRIES ON
KICK RET

EVEN KEEL

JUST DOING MY JOB
WITH LITTLE IMPACT ON
GAME

pepperells

ENVOLVE
THE ENERGY EXPERTS

ELLIS
13

PBS
CONSTRUCTION
NORTH EAST LTD

LOYAL

FINAL TIE
LADBROKES
CHALLENGE CUP
COMPETITION

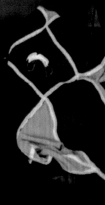

that year built around a formidable defence that had conceded two hundred points fewer than the next team. I was still unable to train but we had an eight-day turnaround and after a while my back began to feel better. By the middle of the week, I even managed to do some light work. I've never liked sitting out training. I needed the exertion of it to make me feel prepared.

There were over 71,000 at the ANZ stadium, fireworks, a guard of honour ... it was quite some occasion. Nobody gave us much of a chance. We had played two exhausting games in the previous fortnight, many of our players busted and patched up. The Dragons, by contrast, had cruised through their first-round match and then had a week off, but we went into the break 12-6 ahead.

The last try of the game came early in the second half, making it all-square with half an hour to go. The momentum was with them, we were out on our feet and hanging on desperately. It seemed only a matter of time before they took the lead, but the clock ticked on and it didn't happen. With ten minutes left, came the moment of controversy. Our winger Lote Tuqiri made a break. Half-tackled, he fell to the ground and Jeremy Smith came in with his knees and smashed him in his ribs. Our physio rushed on, a sure-fire penalty.

While he continued to receive treatment, the big screen in the stadium replayed the incident. We waited for the video referee to confirm the penalty ... and we waited ... and waited. Until he called for a set restart having come to the judgement that the contact was accidental. No foul challenge. Instead of lining up a kick at goal that could have sent us to the Grand Final, shortly afterwards Benji was aiming a punt to touch to gain field position and fluffed it, sending the ball out on the full. They dropped a goal and even though we then had a final clear-cut chance, the dream was all over.

Years later, I had a conversation with Wayne Bennett about the outcome. The penalty we weren't given still hurt me and I reminded him of it but he brushed it away, insisting we still had an opportunity to determine our own destiny. Unbelievably small margins are so often the difference between the end of a season or Grand Final.

I have never been one for dwelling on defeat. I certainly got much better in dealing with the disappointment as I got older, turning it into a positive, motivating me to get better rather than moping around for days not actually achieving anything. I would be low for a while, but after playing in such incredible high-profile fixtures couldn't be too disappointed. By that stage, I only worried about variables I could control. Throughout 2010, I had been proud of my contribution and found myself in a routine that enabled me to be on the top of my game almost every week. It had been a long season, culminating in three games of incredible intensity and drama, and it took its toll. I was absolutely shattered, physically and mentally.

If the play-off defeat in 2010 was disappointing, the 2011 setback was nothing short of heart-breaking. For too long, the Wests Tigers club had lived off the glory of their 2005 success; it was all I heard about when I first arrived. Finally, we had a group of players who were admired for their own performances and style.

As I'd been involved in the Four Nations, I was late returning to pre-season training and, while I rested up, a few of my teammates were sent on the road to do some pre-season promotional work. On their return, they told me about their travels deep into the bush, seeing wild kangaroos, meeting farmers, and I regretted that I hadn't been able to go with them.

The campaign started badly for me, injuring an ankle in the opener against the Bulldogs. At first I was told I would be out for a month but came back too early, struggled with it for weeks, and was then out again for another four. Tim Sheens suggested I take a break and fly back to England. It didn't feel the right thing to do but, after a bit of persuasion I decided it wouldn't be a bad idea after all, to relieve the boredom that comes with being out. It was a great break with family, reminding us what we were missing. A seed was planted.

I ended up looking back on that trip as good management on the part of Wests Tigers. They could see I was feeling low and managed me really well. I came back feeling fresh and determined to make a really big contribution to the rest of the campaign.

On my second game back, in New Zealand against the Warriors, we were well behind, the season hanging by a thread, when I came up with a play I'll never forget; 'doing a Benji' by firing out a reverse flick pass to him with the defence committed. Matthew Johns in commentary said it had to be a fluke. It was totally unplanned but, at that stage of the game and season, it felt like we didn't have much choice but to take a few risks and it worked. We won to put our play-off charge back on track. It would be too easy to call it a turning point, but it certainly felt that way at the time.

The pivotal game came against Manly up on the Central Coast in Gosford, where palm trees ring the ground in a truly picturesque setting. We won it after coming from behind, playing attacking football in short bursts nobody else in the competition could match or defend against. It saw us win eight on the trot and finish fourth.

At that stage of the season, Benji was in the form of his life. Supreme in his mastery of the basics of halfback play, he found time to execute options that were simply breathtaking, often ridiculous and all of them meticulously prepared.

We then gained a measure of revenge for the previous year over St George in the first play-off game at ANZ Stadium. A late flurry of points and we were once again just eighty minutes away from the Grand Final and hot favourites to get there as we prepared to face the Warriors. By half-time in that one, we were seemingly home and dry, 18-6 up and in charge. Yet again, though, the scoreboard began to work against us and the Warriors started to play more desperately to save their season, while we reverted to playing the safety card to cut the risk factor. Nobody wants to be the one who knocks on or makes the mistake that costs the game, but as much as you think you are doing the right thing you are not. Going into the final stages we were clinging on, 20-18.

We were also very conscious of how long was left, the screens around the stadium as visible for the players as they were for the fans and, with two minutes to go, the Warriors kicked to the corner. We fumbled it and Krisnan Inu lunged for the line, came up short, but then dived forward to ground the ball.

The question was, had Tim Moltzen laid a finger on him to make it a double-movement and effectively end the contest? While the video referee deliberated, we huddled between posts. It took him an age, slowing the image down, moving it backward and forward. In that moment the entire season rests in someone else's hands and it isn't a nice feeling. When the word 'Try' came up the sense of utter deflation was desperate, as was the regret.

Those two play-off series only lasted a total of five weeks, but they were the most intense periods of my career. It was exhilarating and, ultimately, bitterly, devastatingly, disappointing. I should be proud to have been involved and I guess I am. But I went to Australia hoping to play in a Grand Final and never got another chance.

15

Just A Job

IT'S ONE OF THE IRONIES of playing professional sport that what was once your dream eventually becomes your job. Often well-paid, but it's a form of employment, nonetheless.

I had the privilege of watching the development of the boys in the scholarship team at Hull. Aged fifteen, maybe sixteen, I saw the fire in their eyes when they were signed by the club. It was like seeing myself as a teenager. At that moment they would play for Hull FC for nothing, forever. That is all they want.

Not long afterwards they won't even notice, as I didn't, when the reality kicks in and you do start to think about money. Player agents come knocking and the business side of the game is suddenly thrust to your attention. What am I worth in relation to what other players are paid? How long should I sign for? Do I need to look elsewhere to further my career, or to get a better deal? The sort of questions they wouldn't have been interested in asking a few years earlier.

Plus, it steadily dawns on them that the club is making money on the back of their effort and pain. Real life creeps in, repayments on the car, a mortgage, a wedding to pay for... and then kids come along. You need to make sure you are getting rewarded properly.

Back in 2003, I would never have imagined that playing for my country would also be work. I'd have done it for nothing. In truth, I never played for England or Great Britain for financial gain, no one does. In this country, international players are better rewarded now, thankfully, but it's still peanuts compared to Australia and nowhere near enough to reward the commitment in terms of time and energy.

Playing for your country in any sport is a huge honour and I am proud to have done so, but after the first few years – and with the exception of a few games – the experiences tend to blur together. We mostly played the same opponents (twenty-six of my thirty-eight appearances were against either Australia or New Zealand), often at the same grounds and usually with the same outcome.

By then, it had become the expectation and, I'm sad to say this, I had probably begun to take my international career for granted. I never presumed that my place in the team was guaranteed. If anyone asked for my thoughts on the end-of-season fixtures, I'd always say: 'If I'm selected.' But I did get picked each year and, by 2009, it had become part and parcel of my life.

I still got that buzz when I received the phone call from the head coach – and if someone had been picked ahead of me I would have been devastated. But the feeling I got pulling my shirt on for the first time in 2003 was never quite repeated. It might have been different if the script had changed now and then, but it never did.

Although we came close to beating Australia, especially in those first few years, we never won a series or tournament against them. In twelve games, I was only on the winning side twice. We were more successful against New Zealand, beating them seven times, but not when it really mattered. The truth is Australia in particular were just too good for us. We often said we were catching them up, but were no closer to doing that by the end of my international career than we were at the beginning.

Four weeks had passed since the end of my first season in the NRL and I was back in England for the 2009 Four Nations. Relaxed and confident, I fairly breezed into the Marriott Hotel in Worsley to report for international duty. I couldn't wait to play against the blokes I had been smashing all year in Australia.

There was also change in the air. Tony Smith was still head coach but there were new faces in the camp; Sam Tomkins, Kyle Eastmond, Richie Myler and Tom Briscoe all made their England debuts in that series. I was the only non-Super League player in the squad at that time, which meant Tony began to speak to me more than ever. It was nice to be able to contribute. I also tried to make myself available for the new guys in the team, to help them settle into the squad.

Beating France in Doncaster wasn't the most memorable game I ever played in, but I could relax, express myself, take a few risks and play a bit more rugby. I won my first Man of the Match award for my country. Next day, we watched New Zealand and Australia draw a high scoring game at The Stoop, in which Greg Inglis went on the rampage. In the days that followed, I found myself being asked in an interview: 'How would you feel about playing centre, to counter the Inglis threat?' I thought that harsh on Lee Smith, expected to line up opposite him, so responded in the only way I knew. 'If I was Lee,' I told the journo, 'I would relish the challenge.'

By half-time at Wigan, Inglis had made three tries, scored one and we were 26-0 behind. When we came out again, Lee had moved to the wing and Eastmond was in the centre. The game was lost but we took it to the Aussies, playing on the edge in a very physical second half. Tim Sheens, the Kangaroos coach, later called some of the tactics 'garbage', but it worked in getting us back into the game.

We scored three times, including my first for a while, getting on the end of a jinking run from Sam and crashing over on the left. When Lee crossed in the final ten minutes to narrow the gap to ten points, we sensed an outside chance of pulling off a shock win, but we had run out of time and paid the price for a poor first forty.

We now needed to beat New Zealand for a place in the final. I had never been a huge fan of playing at Huddersfield, either for club or country. Crowd numbers were never high and the atmosphere a little hollow. But this time there were nearly 20,000 in and, once we got going, the fans really got behind us as we pulled off one of our best wins against the World Cup holders.

Afterwards, we didn't celebrate. We were especially focused on trying to avoid a repeat of what happened in 2004. On that occasion, we had won the group and gone into the final as favourites. It hadn't been a situation we were familiar with and we were blown away by the Aussies by forty points.

In the build-up to the 2009 final, nobody could imagine that happening again – until we lost, 46-16. But there the comparisons ended. Although it was a similar scoreline, the performance was entirely different. It was a gruelling game and, after 50 minutes, we led 16-14 but just couldn't hold on to it. Billy Slater scored soon after, then Brett Morris. We were only six points behind but, rather than digging in and finding a way back into the game, the accumulation of years of disappointment showed. We had no belief that we could turn it around, knew how this ended and were powerless to stop it.

By 2010, I'd had two seasons in the NRL at the peak of my playing powers. Steve McNamara was England coach by then and, in our warm-up and preparation for the Four Nations at the end of the season, I did not feel he was getting the best out of me. I spoke to Sam Burgess, who'd just come through his first season in Australia, and he thought the same, so I collared Steve before our opening game in Wellington. I explained how I was being used at Wests Tigers and how I'd developed my game in the NRL to be more of an attacking threat. If I got more of the ball, I said, I felt I might be able to do greater damage. It wasn't a complaint, more an observation. I must have felt quite strongly because it was not in my nature to question the tactics of my coach. Steve listened politely and made minor adjustments, but it didn't make a great deal of difference.

It was an unsuccessful competition for England and the squad was in transition with lots of withdrawals due to injury. It even left the team without a recognised captain, my name briefly mentioned as a stand-in. It would have been fantastic to lead the team out, even if it was only once. To see my name on a team sheet with (C) next to it would have been special. Steve picked James Graham instead.

After the damp squib that was the 2010 tournament, Steve was determined to use every possible strategy to win the 2011 one. When the squad was named it included a bunch of NRL-based Englishmen in the form of Jack Reed, Gareth Widdop, Chris Heighington and Rangi Chase, whose selection raised a few eyebrows. I had a few concerns myself, especially as I'd faced Rangi when we played the New Zealand Māori the year before! But alongside him in camp there was absolutely no doubt in my mind that he was committed to England, where his career had taken off. Chris, who I knew well from Wests Tigers, was also extremely proud of his English ancestry.

Our first game was against Wales in Leigh, which we won easily, but the one I really looked forward to was Australia at Wembley. It was my first time playing at the national stadium and it evoked all the memories I had of watching Castleford and Great Britain there.

The week before had all the hallmarks of a cup final. We travelled down to our London hotel in good time and were out and about, soaking up the atmosphere. There was a press conference at the Hard Rock Café and I was chosen to represent England, alongside Aussies Johnathan Thurston and Greg Inglis. Afterwards, the media people took us to Trafalgar Square where we had photos taken, much to the bemusement of most tourists and locals.

On Wednesday night, we went to the International Federation awards at the Tower of London. As players, you like to chalk off new experiences and places and we seemed to do a fair bit of it that week. Also at that event were quite a few of my Tigers' teammates. Keith Galloway, Robbie Farah and Chris Lawrence were in the Australian team, coached by Tim Sheens, while Benji was in the New Zealand side. It was good to see them enjoying themselves but, given how we were playing the Australians on the weekend, we observed the usual etiquette of not socialising in the week of a fixture.

The England team in 2011 had an exciting look to it. After years of weakness in the back line, Steve now had a deeper pool of talent from which to pick. At Wembley, it was a compelling first half played in front of a noisy and partisan English crowd of well over 40,000. It was a bruising game too; JP went off early with a knee injury from which he shouldn't really have returned and, later in the first half, both James Graham and I were sidelined with back injuries. Mine was a recurrence of one that plagued the end of my NRL season and I was gutted not to be able to see the game out. It was close at that stage, 12-10 to the Aussies, but yet again they pulled away late on to win, 36-20.

My back caused me to miss the game against New Zealand the following week as well; being a non-playing member of the squad did not suit me one bit. I had too much time on my hands and began to feel sorry for myself. It was now the middle of November and I had been shuttling around between hotels for nearly a month since flying back from Sydney. Some lads I knew at Leeds had started pre-season training, but I hadn't even finished the last one yet.

Elland Road was the venue for the last game. I loved playing there, as I did at Old Trafford and those other big iconic stadiums. There were 34,000 packed in. Just as in so many games throughout my career, we were in contention for long periods. It was 8-8 deep into the second half and then four Australian tries in the final twenty minutes made it look like a hammering.

Fittingly, in the very last play, Darren Lockyer, a man who had tormented us for over a decade, scored the final try. It was his last game in green and gold and it would also be my last appearance against Australia. It summed up my career against them perfectly ... valiant performance, fleeting moments of success, but the Kangaroos ran away with it in the end.

In 2012, after a disrupted NRL campaign, I was glad to be home and didn't expect to be picked for England in the European Nations tournament involving England, France and Wales that followed. The fact that I was probably owed more to reputation than performances. Inevitably, it became a bit of a rout before small crowds and a largely uninterested media. We scored 170-odd points in three games and all that could be said for it was that it got the boys together for a few weeks, leading to another three international caps.

I had watched the introduction of the International Origin Series in 2011 with interest. It was hoped, for a while, that fixtures between England and a side initially called the Exiles might begin to rival State of Origin, a stepping stone for the international team. When it came around in 2013 I had barely returned from my foot injury, so didn't expect to be selected and was surprised and pleased when I was but, once more, it was ill-fated. Early on, I launched myself at Steve Menzies. It was a good hit and he was rocked by the collision. I knew he'd look for revenge and, when it came, he clattered into my back as I stood in the tackle. I had to go off. As I trudged to the bench at the Halliwell Jones Stadium that inauspicious Wednesday night, I didn't know it was the end of my international career.

Even so, I look back on it with pride and satisfaction. There were incredible highs but regular and frustrating lows. Playing for my country was a huge privilege, but it increasingly felt I was doing so disadvantaged. No wonder we lost so many times in the last quarter of games, when we ran out of steam physically and mentally, when you look at our overall workload.

Another big issue facing the UK game is the amount of overseas players in Super League. When I first started I was always drawn to those players and tried to learn everything I could from them, but particularly lads from Australia and New Zealand like Willie Poching, Troy Slattery and David Solomona. I wanted to know everything about how they prepared, how they trained, what they ate. The best athletes in this country play football, while the first choice for those in the Antipodes is rugby league.

Younger players can still learn plenty from working alongside professionals from overseas, although we tend not to get the cream anymore, but the flip side of that is those quota players very often block that youngster's passage, although you can see why it happens. Faced with the threat of relegation and the demand from supporters and sponsors for instant success, owners and coaches often prefer to sign someone with an accent for a quick fix. Even though many have played most of their rugby in reserve grade competitions, they are still more consistent than a youngster who is learning his trade.

However it makes no long-term sense to restrict the development of your own prospects.

The biggest problem is participation at junior level. I asked Isaac recently what he wanted to do when he grew up and he told me he wanted to be a 'YouTuber'. After Rachael explained to me what that was, I was devastated. That is the challenge for sports leaders in this country right now, how to get kids out playing sport. Then, if they show signs of talent, nurturing it to the highest level it can go.

In rugby league, we are nowhere near that at that moment.

16

Awards

AUGUST 2017 AND I AM at Hull FC's training ground, finalising my preparations for the Challenge Cup final. As captain, I'm in high demand from the media.

My phone rings and it's Chris Irvine of *The Sunday Times,* who says he would like to do a feature interview with me. 'It'll be in the paper on cup final day, a big, reflective piece about you, your career and your body. It's a regular feature. We've had dozens of sportsmen and women do it. It's very tasteful.'

I was happy to go along with the request. It's not often that our sport gets such coverage, so anything to promote the game was fine by me. Immediately, I remembered doing something similar while I was at Wakefield. The club put together a calendar which featured some of the players with their shirts off. Ben Westwood and I were chosen jointly as 'Mr August' and I ended up looking like a spotty, scrawny teenager on a lads' holiday.

A few days later, I met Chris and his photographer, Brad, at the KCOM Stadium, where they set up a studio. I was actually really pleased with the shots he took. There was a bit of banter from some of the lads when the article came out, yet as I flicked through the paper, I couldn't believe that this was the same guy who, eighteen years earlier, was so afraid of meeting new people that I had burst into tears outside Wakefield's training ground.

Above all else, it was my time in Australia and the acclaim I earned from some of the most knowledgeable players, coaches, writers and supporters that boosted my confidence most.

The first time I got noticed was in 2003, picked for the Super League Dream Team, a nominal selection made by a panel as to who were the best in their position that season. It was especially pleasing since Wakefield had spent most of the campaign battling relegation. As I lined up alongside the other stars, I felt like a complete outsider, a feeling that returned a few weeks later when I was called up to rub shoulders with them again for Great Britain. As delighted as I was to be chosen, I was glad to get home and be out of the spotlight.

I was back in the Dream Team in 2006, and again the next two seasons while at Leeds. I had only ever wanted to secure the respect of my peers and to be voted into that elite group, this time by my fellow players, was a fabulous way to end each season.

The comparable awards ceremony in the NRL, the Dally Ms, was a different level and a social event in the Sydney calendar. We should have known what to expect when one player's wife asked Rachael, 'Who are you wearing?' As our cab drew nearer to the venue we could see flashlights ... TV cameras ... paparazzi ... red carpet ... there were as many fashion reporters interviewing our wives and girl-friends about their choice of dress and designer as there were rugby league writers. We didn't fancy that, so got the taxi driver to drop us up the street and slipped in by a side door. Next day there was a huge spread in the Sydney papers, with photographs of the stars arriving. There were none of Rachael and me, and we weren't invited again!

I had been nominated for 'second row forward of the year', but was pipped by Anthony Watmough. However, the night ended on a high for me when I was buttonholed by Wayne Bennett. I had never met him before and he made his way over to speak to us before we left. We stood chatting for five minutes or so and he told me how much he admired the way I played the game and congratulated me on the season. That was better than winning any gong.

Weeks later, Wests Tigers held their Player of the Year awards. I couldn't be there, back in England preparing for the Four Nations, but Wayne Cousins, their media manager, had tipped me off that I might be in the running, so I pre-recorded a message. That was the kind of interview I didn't mind doing. The following day I heard that I'd won Player of the Year as well as the Members' Player of the Year. I was incredibly proud and grateful that the efforts of an Englishman had been appreciated. During the internationals, at another gala dinner in Leeds, I was selected in the Team of the Year chosen by the RL International Federation. Again, I was truly humbled.

I used to hate presentation nights, though, especially when there was a chance I might win something. I'd sit there, squirming in my seat, terrified at the prospect of having to go on stage. Speaking in public was my worst nightmare and I always wondered if I could possibly have deserved the nomination. Over the years, I got better at doing Q&As to the point where I could stand there, answering quite confidently, but it wouldn't be my choice.

Season 2009 was probably the high water in terms of personal awards and recognition. I was third in the voting for the Golden Boot, which crown's the world's best player, and selected for the first ever NRL All Stars team chosen by public vote to play against an Indigenous Australian team in a curtain-raiser to the coming season. Being selected by the fans made it even more special, but I had to pull out as it was only a fortnight after Isaac was born.

At the end of 2010, I was present for the Wests Tigers awards night, Player of the Year for the second time running. I clung onto it all the way home, scarcely believing I'd been given it ahead of Benji Marshall who'd just had the year of his life. Unbelievably, it was the same again in 2011, even though I had missed eight rounds due to injury. I'd won the Wests Tigers award for an unprecedented three seasons running – the only hat-trick of my career!

It was during the English late spring of 2011 that I realised our Australian adventure was coming to an end. It was May and I was back home recuperating from an ankle injury. I didn't say anything to my parents, didn't want them to know that we were missing home, but we were. We went back to Australia and got on with our lives there, but conversations about returning came around more often. Living in Sydney was never going to be forever, it had always been a working holiday, but by the start of 2011 a number of things had changed. Firstly, we had Isaac, a one year old now and growing up quickly on the opposite side of the world to his cousins, aunties, uncles and grandparents. Most parents have the benefit of an extended family when bringing up a child, but we didn't and were missing that time together.

Added to which, the novelty of Sydney had worn off a little. We still appreciated its beauty and idyllic lifestyle, but felt we'd seen everything it had to offer. The injury also meant less time with my teammates and too much on the physio's table. Going home, we'd have to sacrifice the outdoor lifestyle we loved and there was a financial risk too, especially as the Aussie dollar had risen in value massively against the pound. But anyway we went back again in October and got married just before Christmas, surrounded by our families and friends, which is what really made our minds up.

We returned to Sydney and, in February, my agent David Howes formally informed Wests Tigers that 2012 would be my final year. I wanted there to be no distractions once I started playing. If this was going to be my last season, I was going to give it everything I had.

Wests Tigers were tipped among the favourites again in 2012 but, behind the scenes, all was not well. Adam Blair was one of the hottest properties in the comp and, in the management's determination to bring him to the Tigers, several long-standing stalwarts of the club were either released or became unsettled. It might still have been a successful year if Blair had reached the expectations everyone had of him but, in truth, he struggled to settle and didn't really fit into the strong group dynamic. He was under pressure to be a different kind of player to the one he was. I didn't think too much about that at the time, but it certainly came back to me later when I signed for Hull and was subject to a similar type of hype Adam experienced.

I already knew Sam Burgess a little bit before he came out to Australia in 2010. We had played together for England a few times and I wasn't at all surprised that he became so successful. It was through him that I came to have dinner with Russell Crowe. Chris

Feather has always been one of my best mates from our time together at Wakefield and Leeds. In 2011 he was living in Sydney, running a gym owned by Russell, and I had arranged to have dinner with him and Sam at an Italian restaurant in Coogee. Earlier in the day, Crowe had called into the gym – Fev having been one of his personal trainers – and asked if he could join us. He insisted that we go instead to his favourite place, a steakhouse in Woolloomooloo. He even had his own table overlooking the harbour. I was a bit in awe of him at first, but he was really down to earth and just wanted to talk about rugby all night. Watching him and Sam interact was extremely funny. They're really good mates who know each other inside out and would bicker like an old married couple.

Whenever I played against Sam there was always added spice. Before the 2012 Heritage Weekend game there was more interest than usual because the England coach, Steve McNamara, was in Sydney to watch us in action, but it turned into a nightmare for all three of us. After just 25 minutes, Sam went down clutching his knee. Having received treatment, he hobbled off not to return. A few minutes later, I was on the floor as well, but had no idea what caused me to suddenly feel such discomfort and pain with every step I took. I had no idea, either, that this most innocuous of injuries would ruin my final season in the NRL.

There had been no impact of any kind. Moving back to my mark, it felt that I had a stone wedged under my foot. I tried to run it off, but each step brought more and more discomfort until it became too painful to run. I called to the bench and our physio, Andrew Leeds, came on to check it out. He had no idea what had caused it either as I hobbled off. As far as Sam and I were concerned, Steve McNamara was a jinx.

I spent the rest of the weekend with my foot in a boot until I could see a specialist. After the scans, he said I had a stress fracture of my fifth metatarsal – the bone which runs along the outside of the foot up to the little toe. It was the same injury that had befallen All Black captain Richie McCaw and it kept him out of action for three to four months. Footballer Wayne Rooney was sidelined for ten weeks with it, so I knew this was going to be a long lay-off.

I was told from day one that metatarsal bones have a very low blood supply, which makes them slow to heal. The surgeon had to insert a small screw into the affected part, take a graft from my heel to help the repair and patch it up. At that stage, he estimated three months before full recovery, so almost half the season.

In the weeks that followed, I set out my recovery plan. I turned up to training every day and did my rehab drills. I kept myself in shape and tried my best to stay positive around the group. I wore a pot for six weeks and was in a boot for another four. When, finally, I was able to take that off, I was still in lots of discomfort, especially in the mornings. The first step of the day as I put weight on it was agony, but by the time my foot had warmed up and I set off for training it didn't feel too bad.

Afterwards it would swell up again and, after a week or so, it wasn't getting any better so I went to see the specialist to make sure it wasn't broken again. He assured me it wasn't, that the pain was nothing to worry about and to be expected. It carried on for weeks. Even after I started playing again, it would swell up afterwards and be sore for days. I just accepted that was how it was going to be.

It was a tough time. I wasn't playing and couldn't train nor do much to help with Isaac either. I began to get under Rachael's feet and was desperate to get back into our old routines. I learned a lot about myself during that time; that I had the mental strength and discipline to stick to a recovery programme, characteristics I would need to call upon again in the coming years.

During the season, the 'forever brothers' culture had been shaken quite badly. The senior players had grown distant from Tim Sheens, even now I'm not really sure why. Nevertheless, when I returned in round 20, the team were still on the fringes of the top eight, with a chance of making the play-offs again.

I had been determined to make 2012 my best season there and, following the injury, promised everyone I'd be back fresh and firing. I achieved neither as I struggled to get back to the form I'd shown in the previous three years. As we tumbled to the bottom end of the table, dad planned to fly out a week after our next game, until I rang to say it was likely to be my last in the orange, black and white shirt.

He changed his plans quickly and came just in time to see it. Going into the weekend, we needed to win and hope for favourable results elsewhere. By the time we kicked off on Saturday night, we knew our exact challenge – to beat second-placed Melbourne by sixty points at home. My final and seventy-fifth appearance for Wests Tigers saw us lose 26-6. We finished tenth, our lowest league placing in my four years at the club.

At the end of the game, despite the realisation that was it, I was delighted that the likes of Cameron Smith, Billy Slater and Craig Bellamy, among others, sought me out to shake my hand. I had arrived in 2008 with no ambition beyond earning the respect of my teammates and opponents, so to have those guys congratulating me on my time in the NRL was the best compensation I could get.

In the following days, there were more nice tributes in the press and from people at the club. At one stage, the NRL projected images of departing players onto the side of the Sydney Harbour Bridge, they do things right there to honour their stars, and it was surreal to see myself up there. But Beau Ryan moved me most. A few weeks after the end of the season, and just before we flew home for the final time, the players came together again for the Player of the Year Awards at La Montage, next door to Liechardt Oval. The place was packed with over a thousand members, sponsors and officials and I got quite choked when Beau got up to collect his award and used his speech not to talk about himself but me.

I'm not sure why his comments got me so choked. Maybe it was because it was my final time with those lads. Perhaps it was because I had managed to finish the season back on the field with them after a horrible year with injury, or maybe it was because he was talking about me not as a rugby player, but as a man and a friend.

I was followed out of the door at Wests Tigers by Beau and Chris Heighington – both of whom joined ex-teammates Andrew Fifita and Bryce Gibbs at Cronulla. I can never be sure what happened next. I knew that the likes of Benji and Robbie were devastated at the sudden and unexpected break-up of the team and voiced their concerns publicly. Not many coaches can survive the combination of a disappointing season, anger from supporters and lack of support from some of your senior players. By the end of September, Tim Sheens had also left his job.

For two years or so we were the most exciting and unpredictable team in the NRL. Those five play-off games will long be remembered by all, and I am hugely proud of my role in them.

For Rachael and I, however, life had moved on. When we arrived in Australia in 2008, we had only been together for a year or two and saw it as a working holiday – a life experience. We expected real life to stand still while we hopped off for a while enjoying ourselves. We didn't quite expect Sydney to have such a profound effect on us and to make such strong and valued friendships. Nor did we think our time there would become such an adventure for our families, who visited us far more often than we anticipated.

By the time we came home, Isaac was two and a half, beginning to talk with a hint of an Aussie accent. I returned to England a much better player, without doubt, but I had grown in other ways too. I was a husband now, and a father. Maturity had crept up on me and I took my responsibilities very seriously. I felt very confident in my strengths as a player, and knew I had a lot to offer my new club in Super League, but it was going to be tougher than I ever imagined.

17

Setbacks

ONCE WE DECIDED TO END our time in Australia, it dawned on me that I didn't have a club to go to. I'd been so focused on the decision there had been no discussion about where I might play.

I faced a decision every bit as agonising as the one that took me to Australia in the first place, but significantly different. In leaving Wakefield to go to Leeds and from there the NRL, I'd been taking a leap likely to make me more successful. This move had the potential to be a step backwards. The quality of football wasn't going to be as high, the money less, and I knew the lifestyle wouldn't match Sydney. I had to make a choice based on challenge and opportunities. I was only 30, there was still time for one more chapter if I got it right.

A few weeks after word got round, I rang my agent David Howes to see how negotiations were coming along, if at all. 'What sort of interest have we had?' I asked. 'Well,' he replied, 'it'll be a bit tough.' My heart sank. Maybe this wasn't going to be such a good idea after all. My mind was racing. What if I couldn't get a top club in England? I was still very ambitious, desperate to play in big games, but there was no going back – I'd already made it public I was returning home.

'Yes,' he continued. 'It's going to be a bit difficult to decide because

I've had interest from every single club in Super League.' I rocked back in my chair. I had hoped to have a bit of a choice, maybe two or three clubs at the top end of the table, but hadn't imagined this. I instantly recalled signing for Wakefield when nobody else was interested. Now I had my pick of the competition's elite and I could make my decision for all of the right reasons. It was a huge relief.

I wanted to be at a club that could compete for trophies, so we started to narrow the options. London and Catalans were out, as that would have defeated the purpose of returning to England to be nearer to family. I also ruled out Salford, Huddersfield, Bradford, Wakefield, Hull KR and Widnes. The Giants were miffed at that and I could understand why. They were to go on and win the League Leaders' Shield in 2013 and felt entitled to make a pitch, but I didn't feel it was a good fit for me and definitely didn't want to waste anyone's time.

I wavered slightly before ruling out Castleford. Playing for the Tigers would have been a nice way to end my career. They were the club I supported as a boy and my family still followed them but, in 2012, they weren't the side they would become a few years later. They also had financial issues so couldn't compete with the other offers on the table. So, with some reluctance, we also turned down Cas.

That left five: Leeds, Wigan, Warrington, St Helens and Hull.

Wigan were very professional throughout. I knew Mark Bitcon, their conditioner, from England duty and he had said some very nice things about me to Kris Radlinski, then their football manager. I was also impressed that they would help me after I finished playing with further education and qualifications. I knew many of their lads from England duty so it would've been a comfortable environment – if that could be said of a Shaun Wane regime – but the big sticking point was travelling over the Pennines every day for training.

Warrington's offer was a good one too but, in all honesty, I didn't give it as much consideration. Although they were a top club, I didn't feel much affinity for them and the detail of their offer and level of interest wasn't the same as at the other clubs I was considering.

St Helens were, from day one, the most attractive from a financial point of view and their owner, Eamonn McManus, told me he would organise a flat for me in Manchester, showing that they understood my concern about travelling. Rachael and I even spent a few hours on the internet looking at properties. Eamonn gave the impression that he really wanted me there, which weighed heavily in his favour, but I was really looking for somewhere nearer to our families.

We'd only just bought our first house together in Wetherby when the Australia opportunity came about and were now excited by moving back in. It came down to a straight choice – Leeds or Hull.

Leeds were the obvious candidates and my first preference. Still successful, I could more or less go back there, hang my training gear on my peg, pick up where I left off and the commute from Wetherby wasn't far. It was definitely the most straightforward choice.

When Gary Hetherington rang me in February 2012 to invite me for a coffee, I knew they meant business. He just happened to be in Australia and we arranged to meet at Darling Harbour. I took the ferry from Chiswick and, arriving early, chose a nice table overlooking the waterfront. But, once again, just as in 2008, when it came to negotiating a contract with Gary, I hesitated. It was easy and just a little *too* convenient. I would be doing the same as before. I needed something different that would challenge me physically and, more importantly, mentally and emotionally, so I listened to Hull.

David Howes arranged a Skype call with their coach Peter Gentle, football manager Shaun McRae and owner Adam Pearson. I knew Peter from my time at Wests Tigers where he had been assistant coach, but little about Shaun and Adam. In truth, I didn't really know much about the club as a whole.

I listened to Shaun and Peter, but Adam impressed me most. 'I am totally committed to making this club great again,' he said. 'It's my money and I'm not going anywhere until we are a top club, competing for trophies. I need you.' He even offered to fly out to Australia, meet me face to face and talk further. I was impressed by his words but conscious that saying those things is the easy bit; there was no guarantee that any of it would happen.

Hull were still a long way short of Wigan, Leeds and St Helens in terms of their competitiveness on the pitch, but that was part of the challenge. If I could play some part in getting them to the level of those three, I would have achieved something with what remained of my career. I wanted to be at the heart of everything that happened at the club, setting the standards and leading from the front and that included the offer of being the club captain. I was motivated by that responsibility.

Slowly, I warmed to the vision. It was a risk but, potentially, could be a highlight of my career. Leeds upped their bid, which would have stretched their renowned pay structure, but in the end it didn't really come down to cash. If it had, I'd have signed for St Helens or stayed in Australia. Not many people say no to Leeds and I'd done it twice. I still had the greatest respect for the club and all associated with them but, ultimately, their continued success worked against them.

The fixture planners must have had a wicked sense of humour, though. On the opening day of the 2013 season, Hull were away to the Rhinos. In the weeks before the game, FC went into overdrive. My face and name were everywhere, T-shirts, posters, flags, scarves, brochures, it bordered on hysteria. I was genuinely worried the fans were expecting me to turn the club around single-handedly.

The narrow streets surrounding Headingley were already busy as our team bus threaded its way through. The Hull supporters were out in force, arriving early to enjoy the build-up. Peter Gentle had transformed his squad in anticipation of yet another return to glory and we were confident of making a good start to the campaign.

There were plenty of cameras around when I stepped off the bus. Supporters wanted selfies and Sky TV were there. It was a bit strange turning into the away dressing room and, although there'd been a couple of pre-season games I still didn't feel I really belonged among the group just yet. I sat down for a few minutes, tried to read a few pages of the match programme, but wasn't really concentrating on it. My thoughts were only on the game and what I needed to do.

I didn't say a lot, there wasn't much to say. I wanted the lads to see their captain calm, exuding quiet confidence, and let my actions do the talking. Peter had inherited a bunch of honest players who just lacked leadership. They had been competitive in 2012 but unable to win those close games that really mattered.

Andy Lynch had been Hull's captain and had – by all accounts –

done a good job. I knew him well having toured with him. Although it had been agreed that I would take over, once I arrived I told Peter that if he wanted to stick with Andy that was okay with me. The team was more important than my ambitions. Peter thought about it for a few moments and then said: 'Okay, but if you don't do it, it won't be Lynchy. I'll get someone else.'

I always knew I was going to like Danny Houghton. 'Mint' had been at Hull for a number of years and I'd always admired the quiet way he went about his rugby, totally dedicated to maximising his talent. He is also one of the most durable I've ever played alongside, there to mop up – a players' player – and his efforts have often been widely overlooked because of his consistency.

Brett Seymour was a different story. Aged 18, he broke into the Brisbane Broncos first team, but couldn't keep himself out of trouble. Discarded by a number of NRL clubs, I never saw him take part in a full training session. He had trouble with his knees and would spend most of his time on the rowing machine or sitting at the back of team meetings on his phone, checking the horse racing results.

Daniel Holdsworth's situation also became a sideshow. He'd come from Canterbury Bulldogs, a very traditional culture where senior players ruled the roost and commanded total respect, and moved to Salford, where we signed him from. Then he met Ben Crooks, son of Hull legend Lee, who broke into the team and never looked back, finished as our top try scorer and earned a place in the Dream Team at the end of the year. Ben was already confident but as his success grew he could not help but wind Holdsworth up. There were times I would watch their exchanges and think it might get out of hand.

They had installed a new pitch at Headingley during the winter. It hadn't yet been fully bedded in, so I chose to play in a new pair of boots with plenty of grip. They had four studs at the front and two longer ones at the back, along the sides. As I pulled them on, I noticed that the stud on the outside of my left foot sat just below the bone I'd injured the previous year but thought nothing of it.

It had been a strange winter. Our last days in Sydney reminded us of why we loved it so much. It was springtime in the Southern Hemisphere, the days were growing longer and the temperature was nudging up every day. We managed to get around a few of our favourite haunts one last time, taking the ferry into Circular Quay and enjoying that view you never tire of – but now we were home.

I'd pack my bag the night before, training gear, change of clothes, usual bits and pieces. The alarm would go and I'd tip-toe around the house in the pitch-dark trying not to wake anyone but, invariably, I would bang into a table leg in the half-light and leave to the sound of Isaac crying. I'd be out of the door by half six, meet the other lads travelling from West Yorkshire at seven and, traffic permitting, we'd pull into the training ground around eight.

We trained at the YPI Sports Centre on Chanterlands Avenue. It wasn't our own facility and we had to share it with local rugby union and cricket teams, while the gym and function rooms were available for public hire. It was odd, in my first week, to be training at a facility that was also playing host to a wake and an Elvis impersonator.

It dawned on me after a week or two that I'd been duped a little. While I was deliberating over which club to sign for, Adam Pearson had sent me a video in which he sold the stadium and facilities. The training ground had looked like a state-of-the-art complex, but it had been one of those artist's impression video fly-throughs and didn't actually exist.

Meanwhile, back at Headingley, it was just after 7.30pm when I left the dressing room, trotted down the tunnel and onto the familiar pitch. The stands were filling up nicely and there was a smattering of polite applause from Leeds fans in the seats around me and cheers from the Hull supporters filling up the open terrace to my right.

I felt relaxed and calm, eager to show Super League what I could do after four years down under. Headingley on a cold, dark Friday night in February was where I wanted to be. I caught sight of some old teammates, the thought of pitting myself against them excited me. I felt a surge of adrenalin, ready to go, and then a 'pop'.

I knew it straight away. When you have had a serious injury, you never forget what it feels like. Gingerly, I walked over to our trainer, Adam Whitney, who was helping with the warm-up. 'My foot's gone,' I told him. The pain on the underside, the difficulty walking on it, was exactly the same as I remembered a year earlier. There was going to be no debut tonight and not for a long time. I hobbled into the empty dressing room and sat down with tears in my eyes. I was absolutely devastated. My teammates and the coaching staff had to come back after their warm-up, but I can't remember what any of them said to me, I was inconsolable. Adam Pearson and then my dad came in and tried to comfort me, but I wasn't having any of it. I managed to take my boot off and threw it at the wall. Outside, the TV coverage was in meltdown. 'Ellis injured in the warm-up,' was the only story in town. After all the expectation, to get injured before I even had a chance to play was as disappointing as it gets.

Around mid-morning the next day, Peter Gentle and Shaun McRae drove me to York hospital for a meeting with Dr Adam Budgeon. It is no overstatement to say he saved my career. Slowly and patiently, he talked me through the scans he'd had taken and it became clear that the operation in Sydney had not gone as well as it might. The insertion into the bone had not stayed in place and each time my foot moved that screw ground into it, which explained the pain I had been feeling every morning for the past twelve months. Worse still, the repeated grinding had carved out a small hollow, which meant it was only a matter of time before it broke again.

After such a detailed explanation, I felt safe in Adam's hands. He booked me in for the operation and as soon as I woke up afterwards I could feel the difference. There was no pain in the bone at all and, in the years that followed, I've never had any more trouble with it.

The mental side of the healing process was the biggest challenge. As club captain, it embarrassed me to sit on the sidelines. I wasn't a big talker, I let my actions do that, so to be injured before the season even began meant I was completely ineffective. I stayed around the players and did my bit, but my impact as a leader was minimal.

By the time I finally made my debut at the beginning of May, on my thirty-second birthday, the team was in the middle of a winning streak that had lifted us to fifth. The game went okay, I just wanted to get through it in one piece. Although Peter and I had spoken about playing me in short bursts, I ended up doing eighty minutes. The foot felt good, I enjoyed being back, but in the coming weeks something preyed on my mind I couldn't quite put my finger on.

Take the Warrington game, my second one back. In the lead-up, I visualised myself smashing into their biggest men, lining them up and putting them on their backsides, making my presence felt and dominating the battle of the packs. Early in the contest, Chris Hill took the ball up and headed towards me. I lined him up, got myself into position and timed my tackle perfectly, putting everything I had into the contact. Bang! I wrapped him up, a teammate came in to finish contact, Hill went down, I grappled with him momentarily. The tackle was complete but Hill was soon back on his feet, playing the ball. He wasn't hurt. My effort had drained no energy from him whatsoever. Unknown to anyone else, I was gutted, shaking my head. If I couldn't make an impact in defence then maybe I could in attack. I took the ball in, made a good hard contact driving through, legs at full power, but there was nothing there.

Nothing special anyway.

Playing every week and participating fully in training means you are constantly getting your body smashed, soft tissue battered, knees in your back, elbows to the back of your head, your fingers and toes trampled on, face bruised and bloodied. These are the day-to-day consequences of playing contact sport with a bunch of blokes who are big, strong, heavy and often careless, clumsy or reckless. Unless you are exposing yourself to that on a regular basis, you aren't battle-hardened or what is frequently referred to as being match fit.

There was a bit more to it. I knew I was a marked man, everyone was looking to get one over on me and my performances certainly weren't matching the pre-season noise surrounding me. Hull weren't getting value for money but there was one way I could repay their faith and that was to step back from the international game. It had been on my mind since I picked up the injury. I hadn't played much decent rugby since the end of 2011 and needed a proper pre-season if I had any chance of being effective come the next season.

In June, I was called up by England to play against the Exiles at Warrington. Most of the guys picked that night would have had their sights set on the World Cup later that year, but if I wanted to keep playing well for another two or three years something had to give.

By now, travelling to Hull was getting the better of me. It wasn't so much the journey, more the sense of disengagement I had with the club in general. The injury and my own lack of impact were part of it, but there was something deeper than that, a nagging sense that I may have made the wrong choice. I was aware they had a long way to go to be competitive on the field, but the culture was a million miles from that at Wests Tigers at their height.

In my first year at Hull, eight of us came from West Yorkshire. None wanted to hang around at the end of the day and consequently nor did anyone else. We'd finish training at four o'clock and, by half past, the ground was empty. It didn't feel that I was part of a closely bonded group. We were just a bunch of blokes who turned up for work and then went home.

With so many new players having come in, by mid-season you'd be expecting to see the squad growing closer, building a team spirit forged over end-of-training coffees or a few beers from time to time, but it didn't happen. Nobody ever really took it upon themselves to sort out the team dynamic and do something to build a camaraderie where the players socialised outside of merely training.

It would be wrong to say the season was a total disaster but even when we did seem to make progress, disappointment lurked around the corner. The highlight was making the Challenge Cup final, my first appearance for a club at Wembley in a competition I revered. As captain, the week leading up was a strange one. The usual buzz and excitement didn't quite envelop me in the same way it had done before and would again. That was because I was nervous at leaving Rachael at home. She was expecting our second child and there was a good chance the baby would arrive with me in London. But I was also affected by the underlying mood at the club. We prepared well and talked confidently but, deep down, there wasn't much belief.

The sense of anti-climax began before the game as the heavens opened. It poured down all morning and all those coming in and out of the team room were talking about was the miserable weather and the state of the pitch; it distracted from the sense of occasion.

We made an error in our first set and were awful in the first few minutes. You can forgive some handing errors in those conditions, but ours were poor. We repeatedly took the wrong options, couldn't build any pressure and, when we had any chance to score, dropped the ball. Worse for me was to find myself watching most of it from the touchline. After 14 minutes, I took the ball in and was tackled by Harrison Hansen. As we made contact, his right side caught my left elbow and, as I twisted around, I heard a ping from my rib cage. I knew straight away – it had happened before – that I had popped a cartilage. I tried to carry on, but it hurt like hell and after a few minutes I went off. Our physio decided that I would be able to return at some stage and gave me an injection to numb the pain. I sat on a training bike to keep warm until I got the call.

One of the worst cup finals ever played out in front of me. To be honest, Wigan weren't much better than us and can scarcely have played so badly to win a trophy. Despite all of that, it was still only 10-0 going into the last few minutes. I returned belatedly, but made no real impression. When Sam Tomkins darted over late on, we just wanted to get off the pitch and go back to our hotel, and, in my case, to be home. Before the game, Rachael went into labour. Afterwards I went looking for Motu Tony, who had my phone in his pocket. 'Things have moved on a bit,' Rachael said, when I spoke to her on the pitch. 'Get back as soon as you can.' I did, stopping only at McDonald's for four burgers on the way up the M1 as hunger hit.

Rachael's labour was quite advanced as I arrived in Harrogate at midnight. She was pacing the floor and couldn't sit still or lie down. Seeing her bed empty, I climbed up and shut my eyes for a moment; it had been a long day. An hour later, I was nudged awake by a nurse.

I had started the day hoping to be holding the Challenge Cup and ended it cradling my beautiful daughter, Eva Willow, instead.

I didn't return to action until the elimination play-off three weeks later. We beat Catalans and at the end of a topsy-turvy season there was still an outside chance we could make it to Old Trafford, but for that to happen we first had to get past Huddersfield.

What happened at the John Smith's Stadium that Thursday night still confounds me. We went into the game well prepared, I had no idea that there was anything else going on in the minds of my teammates. Maybe that showed a weakness of my leadership, an inability to read the mood of the dressing room. I just took everyone at face value that we were all there to win the game. But once it started it was clear that something was wrong. I went to tackle an opponent and a teammate dived in front of me. It resembled nothing we'd practiced. It was like we'd forgotten how to play rugby. Within 14 minutes the Giants led 24-0 and the game was gone.

It was 54-6 at half-time. I'd never played in a game like it nor been so embarrassed on a field. I can't remember what the half-time team talk was like or what was said at the end, it became just a blur. And the final score could have been worse than our humiliating 76-18 hammering. The season was over and not a moment too soon.

There were mutterings about Peter Gentle's job straight away. A few days after the debacle we went on our usual 'Mad Monday', this time to Blackpool, and it was Shannon McDonnell, who Peter and I had both worked with at the Tigers, who got the news first by text. 'Peter's been sacked,' he told me, then half-finished his drink and left. Nobody wants to hear about anyone getting the bullet, let alone someone you know well. It was a sad time. During the evening, I managed to get hold of Pete and thanked him for what he had done for me, told him I felt guilty about letting him down as his captain.

Peter must have ended 2013 with a few regrets of his own. I certainly had mine. I seemed to have jumped out of the frying pan into the fire. The job of turning Hull around was much bigger – and going to take a whole lot longer – than I or Adam Pearson could've imagined. I was in danger of seeing my career fizzle out.

Two days later, Adam appointed Lee Radford as our new coach. The next day, I rang Steve McNamara. 'I can't play in the World Cup,' I told him, ahead of the forthcoming tournament here. I explained that I needed a complete break from rugby. He accepted that and noted: 'You look like you're struggling.' It was said without malice but stung regardless.

I didn't watch much of the World Cup, instead, I put myself on a pre-pre-season programme. If my career was coming to an end, if my best days were behind me, then I was going to leave absolutely nothing behind in finding out. I was going to be the fittest, strongest and best-prepared player at Hull for 2014.

It felt like the last throw of the dice.

Over the previous three seasons, I had missed 38 games through injury. In 2014, I missed just two. That statistic alone justified my decision to step aside from international rugby, but it was my performances during that next season that gave me the greatest pleasure. I was delighted to find that my old power was returning. I was bringing some value to the team and not letting anyone down. However, I wasn't able to change our fortunes on the pitch and we found ourselves in twelfth place by mid-August.

Two teams were to be relegated at the end of the season. London were rock bottom and Bradford several points adrift of us as well, but they were appealing a points deduction. If successful, they still had a chance to overtake us. With four games left, our visit to Odsal against them was crucial. Win and we would probably be safe. Lose and we were in danger. Prior to the game, Adam spoke to the players and laid it on the line. At half-time, Radders really tore into us, calling us liars for not being true to our pre-game promises, but it didn't make much difference, we were never really in it.

Thankfully, we managed to win two of our last three games and Bradford's appeal failed. We stayed up but, personally, I did feel like I was slipping into anonymity. What helped, though, was the Rugby Football League awarding me a three month testimonial for service to the sport rather than being ten years at a particular club.

I owe a great deal of gratitude to Peter and Glen Smurthwaite, Andy 'Wolfie' Phalen and Carol Bilton for the time they put into organising the various events, the first of which was 'Hull FC Factor'. I'm not sure I have ever been more out of my comfort zone than when I sang 'I Got You Babe' alongside Hull boxer Tommy Coyle on the stage at the City Hall, but it was great fun.

There was a testimonial game against Wakefield played as a pre-season warm-up and the finale was a Captain's Dinner attended by lots of ex-Hull skippers including Johnny Whiteley, Vince Farrar, Steve Norton, Karl Harrison and Richard Swain, who flew over from New Zealand. That more than anything brought home to me the privileged position I was in. Meeting them underlined that I was just the latest in a long line who had held the honour. I probably hadn't seen it that way until then and it recharged my enthusiasm.

18

Soul Searching

July 2015
Craven Park, Hull KR

MARC SNEYD HAS KICKED LONG downfield and we've put in an aggressive chase, pinning Rovers inside their 20-metre line. I am the last man out of the tackle and bust my backside to get back ten metres so I can be the first one again leading the defensive line.

I turn to push off, then... twang! It feels like a truck has run into me. The impact sends pain rippling up my back and through my body as I lie, crumpled, on the floor. I assume it must be one of the Rovers' players, running back onside and not looking where he is going, but there is nobody there. The physio jogs on. 'Can you move your foot?' he asks. I look down. My left one is hanging limp off the bottom of my ankle. 'Achilles,' the doctor says.

They strap a medical boot to my lower leg and I hobble to the side of the pitch. I'm not going to be stretchered off, not at Craven Park in the derby. They take me to Hull Royal Infirmary where what we already suspect is confirmed. At the age of thirty-four, time takes on a new significance.

'Nine months,' is the verdict on the likely recovery time, 'maybe twelve.' That's it. This is the end. It's all over.

I was in a dark place for those first few days. Nine months out, perhaps a year? I could go through all of the recovery, rehabilitation, and for what? There wasn't much for me to do around the team and the lads kept a respectful distance for a while. They had their own struggles, failing to make an impression in the new Super 8s format and ending the season on a low. Then, out of the blue, my phone rang. It was Mark Flanagan.

We'd been together at Wests Tigers and now he was at St Helens, where he was a teammate of Ade Gardner who had gone through similar and got back in four months. I messaged Ade and he told me the full story, all about his surgeon, an expert in the field, and recovery. The conversation gave me hope. I made an appointment straight away in Manchester and booked in for the operation.

Injuries were always an occupational hazard given how I played, but it wasn't until I hit thirty that they became a recurring, worrying issue. As a result of a couple of decades of hitting big blokes with my ribs and being hit by them in return, they were already in a bit of a state – and that was before I ran into Remy Casty.

Early in the second half at home to Catalans in 2015, I drove the ball in hard at the big French international, who wrapped himself around me, squeezing my upper body and putting huge pressure on my midriff. There was a loud pop as I heard the cartilage go. The pain was so intense I couldn't get my breath, there was no position I could put myself in that didn't hurt like hell. Physio Jamie Moseley rushed on but I couldn't even speak and, seeing my discomfort, he started to lead me off the field. It was so bad that I felt my legs go and I had to kneel down for a moment.

I couldn't lift my arms, they had to cut my shirt off me. Someone drove me home and gave me more painkillers, but I couldn't sleep or even lay down properly. The only way I could get any comfort was to sit upright in an armchair, so that was the position in which I managed to grab a few hours of fitful rest.

I woke up next day with a headache. The amount of pain I was in had Jamie worried and he immediately sent me off to Liverpool to see a specialist in rib and sternum injuries. He said I'd fractured a rib and torn the cartilage but at least another seven of them hadn't healed properly, illustrated by various bumps and lumps on my rib cage. Bits of calcified bone that had healed themselves into abnormal shapes traced the story of a decade and a half on the battlefield.

'But that's not all,' he said, voice dropping a level at this latest prognosis. 'You have displaced your rib cartilage, but instead of it flicking outwards, as is usually the case, this piece has gone inwards and it's resting on your heart. It can't do you any major harm, but that would explain why you were in such agony.'

I look back on this catalogue of injuries and discomfort now with detached circumspection. I knew exactly what I was getting into and enjoyed every bit of it. Playing rugby gave me the best experiences of my life. I might feel differently as I get older – I'm aware that I have taken out a mortgage on my body which will not be repaid until later – but, for the time being, I have no regrets. There were always risks and I am comfortable with that.

In the final few games of the 2015 season, 'Radford Out' banners started to appear around the ground at home matches. After three years at Hull, we seemed as far away from winning something as ever. Even in those darkest moments, however, the commitment of owner Adam Pearson was not in doubt. He told everyone Radford was going nowhere and backed him with a wave of new signings.

Come mid-December, I was braving the cold and damp at the County Road training ground, learning to gently run again. It was the first time I'd had my boots on in five months and been on grass. As I walked out of the changing room I was gripped by doubt. It felt good to be moving my body forward with ease. Suddenly, I heard a shout, then a cheer, then more voices – all aimed in my direction, a welcome back from my teammates. I knew this wasn't where it was going to end. I was going to play again, no matter how long it took.

'We've got to do something about this,' Danny Houghton says, as we walk down the tunnel at Widnes the following March, ahead of the rest of our downcast side, having just been given a hammering.

He is right. It can't continue.

We walk calmly into the changing rooms under the main stand. Nobody speaks, the usual scene after a defeat. Players start kicking off their boots, ripping at their strapping, while staff scurry around fetching drinks and tidying up. 'Can we have some time to ourselves, please,' Danny says, in a voice that sounds like it needs listening to. 'Can everyone but the players leave, please.'

Soon, there's no one in there but the team that has just lost 46-6. It doesn't matter that this is the best start to a season Widnes have had for years, or that the win puts them top of the league. We were shocking, completely fell apart. Worse, we gave up the fight.

Mark Minichiello, a seasoned Aussie, speaks as well. There are no dramas or arguments. 'If anyone has got any problems then they need to speak up now, preparation, coaching, each other, then let's hear it,' he says. Nobody speaks, a few shrugs and headshaking. Deep down, we know there are no excuses. 'The problem is with the blokes in this room and it's only us that can fix that up, starting now,' Houghton adds. And that's that.

It wasn't the most enjoyable return journey. Nobody spoke on the bus, lost in their own thoughts. I don't think any of us thought we would make headline news, though. It wasn't about the players shutting the coaches out, it was just about ourselves.

But that wasn't how the headlines saw it.

A fortnight later, the fruits of that discussion were evident when we came from 20-0 down in the derby at Craven Park, edging it in the closing minutes to pandemonium and delirium from ourselves and our fans. There is no better feeling than winning a game from such a hopeless position. We weren't celebrating the performance, it was our character we were proud of. We had become a much more durable side. Even when we didn't always play well we were tougher to beat and had found a way to win the close games.

It had taken longer than I'd originally hoped, but in my fourth year at Hull it looked like we were finally on the brink of success. If there was a chance we might win something I wanted to be part of it, so was keen to extend my contract again to 2017. At the age of 35, I knew I wouldn't be offered the same deal I was on when signing for the club in 2012, but I was happy with the proposal and the deal didn't take long to sort out.

Frank Pritchard had arrived as one of the biggest names in the

Never the Easy Option

NRL and his influence on the squad was immediate. He is a proud man who takes his rugby seriously. In those early weeks, when we really needed to believe that 2016 would be different, he was at the heart of that mood. Great to be around, his enthusiasm is infectious.

Our cup run came to public attention when we convincingly beat St Helens live on BBC television in the sixth round. I even managed a try. The victory, at Langtree Park, was our eighth in nine games. We were unrecognisable from the side that gave up at Widnes and second in Super League, behind Warrington on points difference.

In the next round we drew Catalans at home, managed the game well and won comfortably. The victory against the Dragons was our tenth on the trot and by now the lads couldn't wait to be in each other's company. During breaks, the games of pool or darts became more raucous, nobody skulked away on phones. At the end of each session they hung around, everyone wanting to be part of what was building. By the end of the regular season, we were top of the table.

Of all the games in which I've played, few were more satisfying than the Challenge Cup semi-final victory over Wigan. There was a great sense of occasion as we arrived at the Keepmoat in Doncaster. It was a warm Friday night, perfect for rugby, and the black and white fans had travelled in great numbers, massively outnumbering the Wigan followers. We felt genuinely confident in a way I had not previously experienced while playing for Hull.

Within minutes of kick-off, I knew – you just do – that this was going to be one of those games... close, hard-fought, bruising. Until that season I'd never felt I played particularly well in big club games. At Leeds and Wests Tigers, I'd often not needed to, surrounded by great players who took such responsibility away. I just had to do my job. But by 2016, I reckoned the responsibility was mine and I was ready to rise to it. I played well that night, felt strong and dominant, almost invincible. You could see that when I broke through in the first half, stepped around Sam Tomkins and plunged for the tryline.

My lack of celebration probably influenced referee Ben Thaler, who signalled 'no try' on the field but referred it upstairs. Looking back at the footage later, I thought it was a try but not quite enough evidence to overturn Thaler's decision and so, not for the first time, my modesty had probably cost me. It didn't matter. We closed it out and the joy on the pitch and in the stadium was incredible when the hooter went. We'd been behind for long stages of the first half, but it hadn't bothered us. We'd learned that we could win from anywhere provided we hung in long enough. We were going to Wembley.

Everything at the club seemed to go into overdrive and, at that stage of my career, I didn't mind all the extra interest and excitement, I was in my element. We headed south on the Thursday, cheered by a crowd of supporters as we left the KC Stadium. The coach journey, although long, reminded me of those trips I'd taken to Wembley with my dad and uncles as a kid. I never mind being away from home on such occasions. I like the time and space to get myself ready for what is to come.

We stayed in a lovely hotel in St Albans and wanted for nothing. On Friday, we went for our walkabout on the pitch. The stadium and Wembley Way were all decked out with huge pictures of the players and, even at the age of 35, it felt unreal to see myself up there.

I had often struggled to get my preparation right for big matches and with keeping my emotions in check. This time I felt much more relaxed. I slept well and was calm and unruffled as we went through our final preparations the following morning, but something must have changed once we reached the stadium. Watching it back later, I looked very obviously nervous during a BBC interview I did with Robbie Hunter-Paul in the dressing room beforehand.

Once the game began I was wired, edgy and overly hyperactive, intensely aware of every moment and incident. There was a break in play after fifteen minutes and our conditioner, Paul Hatton, who ran the messages on game day, came sprinting on. He took one look at me and was shocked. 'Gaz has gone,' he told our assistant coach, Andy Last, over his radio. The idea had been for me to play 20-25 minutes before coming off, but this was earlier and caused a real headache with the substitution strategy.

However, with the game slipping away, I was back in the 50th minute rather than the hour mark, as planned. We were 10-0 down and the noise from our supporters, which had been deafening, had begun to ebb away. I'd calmed down and began to impose myself on the game. We stayed in it and Mark Sneyd's 40/20 gave us and our fans a lift. You could sense the game was turning. Within seconds, Sneyd launched a kick to the corner and Mahe Fonua scored. Jamie Shaul went over seven minutes from time and we were in front.

Warrington had all the possession. The pressure was building in those final stages and, with a couple of minutes left, I felt we had gone. The emotion of taking the lead had drained us and they were all over us again. I missed Joe Westerman, they got another set, and I saw the scenario unfold. Ben Currie had the ball in his hands, the ground was damp, and when he hit the floor it seemed certain his momentum would keep him moving to win the game for the Wolves in heartbreaking fashion for us. That Wembley promise was ebbing away and it was my fault for failing to make the crucial tackle.

Many years later, in my first few days as assistant coach at Hull, I got the players together and spoke to them about what became known as 'Tackle 52' – pulled off by Danny Houghton – which saved the day. 'It happened because of all the hard work Danny put in for years to get fit, to stay strong, to practise his technique, so that if the situation ever required it he would be able to do what he did, the culmination of all of those years invested in staying in peak physical condition. That's the level of consistency you need to succeed and that's why Danny's tackle will now be part of Challenge Cup history.'

The hooter went and I almost stumbled to my knees in relief. The tension fell away and joy surged. I took some deep breaths and tried to slow everything down. Normally I can't remember one game from the next, but was determined that wouldn't happen now. We hugged, jumped around and couldn't believe what we had done.

Then, as I led the boys up through the stand, I took each step slowly, savouring every moment. At the top, they take you aside momentarily, beneath the Royal Box. The only words I could hear were those in my head from David Topliss about what it would mean to be the first Hull skipper to lift the Challenge Cup at Wembley after so many disappointments, something Adam had reiterated when wanting to sign me.

If it were a movie, it would be in slow motion with all of the noise in the stadium muted. Danny was almost jumping out of his skin next to me, whacking me on the chest. Scott Taylor looked like he was going to bounce out of the stadium. I lifted the cup to my lips, give it a great big kiss, and then paraded it again high over my head. There was ticker tape flying, 'A Sky Full of Stars' blaring out. I can still see the lads going berserk to my left and me screaming for joy, leaping up and down now, but it's just me, I'm not thinking of anyone else. I can't hear a thing for the noise. I'm just loving that moment. I could burst with pride and happiness.

As the Cup disappeared into the arms of our teammates, Danny and I paused at the end of the balcony and had a proper man hug. I'd grown close to him; he's a guy I can open up to. We've shared a lot at Hull and those few moments on the balcony were special.

Back on the pitch, it was time to share our celebrations with each other, the staff and joyous supporters, and then we were back in the dressing room, singing 'Old Faithful' for all we were worth. I had to tear myself away to do the media. By the time I got back most of the lads were changed and on their way to the Great Hall, to meet their families. The enormous room was full of dignitaries, ex-players and sponsors and I was dragged from pillar to post when all I really wanted to do was be with Rachael and my parents.

On the bus, we had a few beers and then, once we got back to the hotel, there was a free bar all night. To be honest, though, like most of the lads, I was just exhausted. Seeing my family was special and I think my dad had a bit of a tear in his eye when we met up and had a hug. You almost feel obliged to get drunk and have a party, but after a couple of hours I just craved my bed.

Some of the things that happened in the immediate aftermath will stay with me forever. The next day we went out in Hull and were mobbed by supporters wherever we went. I doubt I bought a drink all night. We finished in The Piper Club and totally took the place over. Mahe Fonua and some of the others jumped into the DJ booth and we had one hell of a time. I managed to take a few seconds at one point to stand back and watch them all enjoying themselves. I wanted to take it all in, savour every moment.

It's an unwritten rule that wives and girlfriends don't expect to see you for a while after a Cup win, so the next day we did it all again.

We met up at the KC Stadium and boarded an open-top bus for a parade of the city, finishing at the Queens Gardens in the city centre for a big get-together with supporters. When the bus reached Hessle Road, we were in the very heart of black and white territory, a place where supporting Hull FC is a way of life. The bus turned a corner and I spotted a group of old folk outside a nursing home. Some were in wheelchairs, or leaning on their walking frames, but they still had their black and white colours on. I almost choked up at the thought of those old men and women waiting all their lives to see Hull bring the trophy back from Wembley. There was so much emotional connection to us that day.

Some of the lads went out again that night but, for me, that was enough. I find it hard to summarise how I feel about that Cup win even now, and my part in it as captain. It was such a central part of the vision sold to me when I signed in 2012 especially, and even more poignant when I thought my career might be over, twice.

There was an interesting epilogue to 2016.

At some point in those first few days of October, when we were doing the rounds of awards dinners, I had a voicemail from Wayne Bennett, recently appointed as the national coach in quite a coup. My first thoughts were that he was going to ask me to come out of retirement and play for England. It had been my best season for years and I had picked up a lot of personal accolades, including Dream Team selection again. Perhaps he felt I could still do a job for him? I also heard Sean O'Loughlin had picked up an injury and would probably miss the Four Nations.

Truth is, I never actually retired from international rugby league. Back in 2013, I withdrew from the World Cup but didn't walk away. I'd explained that to Steve McNamara and he never considered me for selection again. By then I was more than happy concentrating on club rugby, but now Wayne's call intrigued me.

I mulled it over and left him a message saying if his call was about playing, I'd now definitely stood down from the international arena, formally announcing to him my retirement, but he never returned it. In the conversations we've had since, he has still never told me why he wanted to speak to me.

If I look back on my international career, I never really played to my full potential. I had some good games, but a lot of the time I was picking up the flak. The mentality that served me so well at club level let me down a little bit in the Test arena.

19

Repeating and Retirement

ALTHOUGH MY BODY WAS STRUGGLING, I always felt I would play well into my thirties. At 31, I had no qualms about signing a three-year deal with Hull, nor with extending it to play in 2016 and again for 2017. But as I began that season I had not yet made up my mind whether it would be my last, even if my knees were telling me that it should be.

There had been a few conversations with Adam Pearson, which had laid out a plan. I would play in 2018 then call it a day and step into Motu Tony's shoes as Hull's football manager; it seemed like a seamless transition into life after playing.

It was at Wakefield on the opening weekend of the 2017 season, ankle deep in mud and freezing cold, that I first asked myself: 'Why am I still doing this?' The following week, at home to Catalans, I was forced off with concussion. That's not the start to a season you want when you're nearly thirty-six and I missed two games as a result.

In April, we produced our best performance of the season to beat Castleford, but I caught an elbow from Junior Moors right into my sternum. It was the kind of pain I have only experienced a few times in my career, totally debilitating. But the game was in the balance, they were camped on our line and so I had to carry on. Every contact was excruciating, but we held on for a brilliant win.

Afterwards, I couldn't move. There had been ligament damage behind the sternum, which complicated the recovery. The projected four weeks absence came and went and I was nowhere near ready to return. With these kinds of injuries there is always the option of playing through the pain barrier with painkilling injections, but I was not going to do that, not after my experience during the play-offs with Wests Tigers. My back has never been the same since.

Besides, it would inhibit my game and if this was going to be my last season, I wanted to make sure that, when I did return, I'd be fully fit and able to finish it properly. It was during this period when I seriously began to think that this could be my last season. Not only were the injuries more frequent but the recovery period after each one was frustratingly long. Everything pointed in one direction.

Throughout my career, I had always felt really focussed on the morning or afternoon of a game. I knew exactly what I had to do. I could visualise my role. It was sharp and clear. But in those weeks, it had been different. I could only describe it as 'fuzzy'. It lacked clarity, yet playing rugby league was the only job I had ever had. What would I do to support my family?

Hull played in fits and starts in 2017. It was enough to keep us around the top four, but it didn't seem likely that we would be challenging for the Super League trophy. At least we were still in the cup, brushing past Catalans and then beating Castleford in the quarter-finals in another thrilling game at the now KCOM stadium. I had something to set my sights on – a semi-final against Leeds for another shot at Wembley, but was still unfit. Spring became summer and the weeks dragged on. Nobody at the club spoke to me about a further contract extension, but we set a target. Once I had three games under my belt, we would sit down and talk.

In July, I had a hit-out in the reserves against Halifax – my first game for three months. We won, they named me Man of the Match and, afterwards, the pain was manageable. I was happy with that and now had the luxury of an eight-day turnaround before our meeting with the Rhinos.

The Challlenge Cup brought out another level of performance from us. We had grown used to having it around the place, taking it out and showing it off. Although we won the semi comfortably in the end, we had to work hard; the points we scored in the second half came after we had earned the right to play that kind of football. Finally, it felt like I was at a top club, that we deserved to be playing in the biggest games and began preparing to go to Wembley again.

This time, all the arrangements were very smooth. The club just copied everything they had done in 2016. Same hotel, same personal butler for Mark Minichiello, everything. Meanwhile, for me, it was decision time. We won our next two games, against Salford and then a thrilling encounter in the pouring rain at St Helens. That 8-6 victory put us top of the league and I felt good. Wembley was just around the corner and we had a chance of making the Grand Final. I still had that fear of the unknown, though, an apprehension of what retirement would be like. Although I was still wavering, by the start of the following week, I had made my mind up. I was going to play on – but circumstances had changed.

Hull would still offer me a deal but, given the injuries I'd had, they imagined I'd play far less – and be paid commensurably. That's not how I saw my involvement. If I was going to put myself through pre-season again, I wanted to play as much as my body would let me. I met Adam a couple of weeks before Wembley. He wasn't feeling well and didn't say much, only told me there was also a change with regards to the football manager's role. Motu Tony was going home early, the club needed to appoint someone to replace him sooner than expected. The job was mine, if I retired. Were I to play on, he would have to find someone else and there was no guarantee that there would be anything for me at the end of it.

I've always had a good relationship with Adam. He told me that he didn't want to be the man who retired me and I believed him, but it still knocked me sideways. He was adamant that there was nothing more he could do. In the moment, I felt let down by the club, rail-roaded into finishing playing. We agreed I'd take a couple of days to decide. I'd rarely discussed rugby with Rachael but this was different. This wasn't just a matter of which club I played for, it affected what

I did for the rest of my life. She told me to do whatever would make me happiest.

Next, I spoke to my dad. He is a proud man and I expected him to say, 'Stuff 'em son, go somewhere else. Don't let them stop you playing if you want to.' I knew how much he enjoyed my career and expected him to persuade me to crack on, but that isn't what he said.

'We've had so much enjoyment out of you,' he began. 'The whole family has been all over the world watching you and loved every minute of it. Now's the time to do what's right for yourself.' It was his way of telling me to retire and that was all I needed to hear.

I called Adam, told him my decision and we moved fast to get the news out. The announcement was formally made in mid-August and, as I spent the day talking to the media, I grew more and more comfortable with the decision. I knew there was no going back and felt like a huge weight had been lifted off my shoulders. Now that it had been made, providing I could avoid injury for the next six or seven weeks, I would retire on my own terms. Hopefully, if the stars were aligned, at Old Trafford.

We played Huddersfield the following night and, on the morning of the game, all the old sharpness came back. It was my 450th career game and I was given a terrific reception. I even scored the game's opening try, but that was as good as it got. We slipped behind by half-time and then lost heavily. But all of that was behind us the following week when we headed down to London.

We travelled to Wembley in a different frame of mind to 2016. We were the cup holders and went into the game as favourites. When I was a kid, I used to wonder whether the Wigan players ever got bored of winning at Wembley during their phenomenal run in the 1980s and 'nineties. All I can say is that the second time around is, if anything, even more enjoyable. You know what's coming, which means you can relish it more.

The hours before a big game are incredibly intense and often very emotional, making sure everyone understands the significance of the occasion. On the morning of the 2016 final, we'd watched a video in the team room which showed some of our finest moments from a great season. But in between the action clips there were also some pre-recorded messages from our family members. We didn't know about that before seeing it and it really struck a chord.

In 2017, when the playing shirts were handed out, instead of getting an ex-player to do it we shared the job between us, handing our shirts to each other. Once again, it gave us a chance to show how much we valued one another. By the time we were done and heading off to Wembley, it felt like nothing could stop us.

It had taken a long time, but I also found myself better able to manage my own emotions in a major game. In 2016, I had been huffing and puffing so much with nervous energy I was knackered after ten minutes. This time, I took it in my stride, felt much more comfortable and, as a result, was more dominant in everything I did for my team.

Although the final score was close, we controlled the match in a way that we hadn't the year before. However, in the final stages, we could still have lost it. Leading 18-10 going into the last ten minutes, Wigan began to play more expansively, demanding a reaction from us. When Joe Burgess scored with seven minutes to go, our nerves were on edge. Those final plays seemed to last an eternity and, in the last minute, as they moved the ball to their left, they were in the clear with Burgess again racing down the wing. I was in line with the final pass and knew it was a long way forward, even so it was a relief when I saw that the referee had called it.

Winning in 2017 was different, but no less gratifying. The first success was joyous relief, the second more satisfying. With Hull in 2016, there was disbelief at what we had done; it was surreal to walk up the steps and lift the Challenge Cup. The year after, we were all aware of it a little more and, in doing so, perhaps the enjoyment was even deeper. Comparing the two is like trying to decide which of your kids you love most. I'm incredibly fortunate to have lifted the cup twice and to do so at a time of my life when I was mature enough to appreciate it.

Unfortunately, in 2016, Hull City Centre was getting ready to become the City of Culture and the area around the City Hall was being redeveloped, so our celebration was moved to the Queen's Gardens. But, in 2017, we took the cup to the City Hall balcony. I don't think anyone enjoyed it more than me. One by one, we were called to the front. I was the last, bringing the cup to the edge and holding it aloft to thousands of supporters that had come to welcome us home. What a way to begin bringing the curtain down.

So confident were we after winning the cup that our thoughts immediately turned to making the Grand Final for the first – and only – time since 2006. We had to get straight back on the horse and avoid the mistakes we had made the previous year when our season had run out of steam. I refrained from over-celebrating and worked as hard as ever in the days building up to our next league clash. We had slipped to fifth in the standings and barring Castleford, who were miles clear at the top, there was very little between the sides in the play-off places, so every game counted. I remember looking at our remaining fixtures which included, Leeds, Wakefield and Castleford ... it was going to be a very fitting end, a farewell tour of my old stomping grounds.

First up were the Rhinos. It was ridiculous that we were asked to play on a Thursday, just five days after the Challenge Cup final. That kind of scheduling totally devalues the players and the sport in general, but we put in a good performance, stayed in the game until late on, before losing 38-26. I hadn't given any thought to there being any repercussions from it, despite being sin-binned in the first half.

It happened after 25 minutes when I found myself tackling Stevie Ward. As we hit the ground I landed on top of him, but then someone came into the tackle behind me, forcing me further down onto him. I was aware that I had landed on his neck but there was nothing I could have done about it. I rolled away but he stayed on the floor. Straight away, I could see referee James Child talking to the video ref, reaching into his back pocket and saying something about it being a crusher tackle and brandishing a yellow card.

It was frustrating but I'd forgotten about it until Monday morning when head coach Lee Radford told me I had been charged with a Grade B offence, which carried a two-game suspension. I potentially only had three matches left before I retired. I had a choice, I could take the early guilty plea – even though it had been completely unintentional and unavoidable – and cop a one-game ban, or stick to my guns, wait for the hearing, and hope to get away without suspension, risking a doubled ban if I failed.

I took the EGP, sat out the fixture with Wigan, and got myself ready for what was now a must-win game against Wakefield in what would be my last home game at the KCOM Stadium before I retired. I was delighted the club invited a large number of family members over as guests. Rachael and the kids, my sisters and wider family came to a lot of my games but rarely together, so it was nice to have them all there.

I was given a terrific reception by the Hull fans. Although I would rather have just turned up and got on with the game, I was quite touched by the guard of honour given to me by players of both sides. Wakefield were still hopeful of squeezing into the top four and gave us a real game, leading at half-time. It was 12-12 as we went into the last ten minutes until I crashed over, writing my own script, to score the winning try and end up with the match ball afterwards.

We needed to beat Castleford in the final game of the regular season to be sure of a top four finish. With top place guaranteed, the Tigers decided to leave out most of their regular first team squad, making our task much easier. Although it was something of an anti-climax, we weren't complaining when we won easily.

We finished third and faced one more sudden-death game in the race to Old Trafford, back at Leeds. It was an emotional night all round. Whatever the outcome, it was going to be the last game at Headingley for Danny McGuire and Rob Burrow, and I had been asked by Leeds if I would join the guard of honour for them before the game. It was an incredible thing for them to offer a member of the opposition and, at first, I thought it would be great. Then it dawned on me that I had already had my moment and the night rightly belonged to Danny and Rob. The sense of something coming to an end hung heavy in the air.

I played that game like it was my last. I was going to leave nothing out there. Deep into the second half, with us trailing by a few points, I must have been showing signs of fatigue. It was well past the time when I would normally be substituted but Danny Houghton was yelling in my ear: 'You're not going off. We're still in this, you're not going off!' And I didn't, not for ages. I probably played for longer in that game than any other for years, I was enjoying it so much. I felt like a young man again, just had boundless energy that night.

I still struggle to watch the final try they scored and the opportunities that we had to stop it. It could have been my fairy-tale ending, but it wasn't to be. It was, however, the perfect one for Danny and Rob, two of the sport's finest. I really enjoyed their ultimate success and they totally deserved to end their glorious careers with Grand Final rings. If I wasn't going to win it, I couldn't wish for a more deserving pair to play their final game on the biggest stage.

There is a lovely photograph of Danny and I leaving the pitch at Headingley with our arms draped across each other's shoulders. After the medals and the success, it's those relationships and friendships that always mattered to me and do so even more now.

After the game, I felt only relief. It was done. All of the worry and anxiety was over and I could let go. Every year, it had taken so much out of me that the prospect of not having to go back to training in six weeks was very appealing indeed.

I was incredibly fortunate that I already had a job lined up. I wasn't really sure what it entailed, nor whether it was what I really wanted to do, but for now it gave some purpose to the weeks to come and made it easier to come to terms with the fact that I wasn't a rugby league player anymore.

But I hadn't reckoned on how much I was going to miss playing. How badly I would adjust to being an office employee. Or how the yearning for the challenge would prove too strong to resist and would eventually draw me back.

20

Wrong Place, Wrong Time

THURSDAY 7 DECEMBER 2017

I'm in the office today, a few weeks into my new role as Hull FC's football manager and it's quiet. Sent an email to the RFL. Waited for reply. Watched the lads train.

FRIDAY 8 DECEMBER 2017

Got a reply to the email I sent yesterday. Read it straight away and replied. Watched the lads in the gym.

Before he left, I asked Motu Tony what being a football manager actually entailed. 'It's hard to describe,' he told me. 'But you'll have plenty to do.'

Four weeks into my new role, that was not my experience.

I didn't really know what I was meant to be doing and, as for the few things that were occupying my time, I had no idea whether I was doing them right.

I looked forward to the new year and the start of the season. Maybe then things would pick up.

TUESDAY 16 JANUARY 2018

It's 8.00am and I'm pacing my kitchen floor looking at my watch and phone. If all goes to plan, in fifteen minutes, an Acklams coach will pick up the Hull team at the County Road training ground. I'm at home, shitting myself. This behind-closed-doors training game at Leigh is the first 'fixture' in which I've played a part in organising. As nervous as I am, I'm glad to have something to do.

Lee Radford has asked if I can sort out the transport and food somewhere near the ground, where we can eat beforehand. It doesn't sound like too big a job, does it, what could possibly go wrong? I contact our transport company, confirming the date, pick-up time, where we're going, where we're stopping, and what time we want bringing back. Straightforward. I check it again. Sorted.

I find a place near Leigh Sports Village, a pub with a good menu, and book tables for the players and staff. I put it all in an email but, after a few days, still haven't received a reply. Slightly worried, I ring them and they confirm that the booking is organised, no problem. They just need me to email the food pre-order, which I do. After another few days, I still haven't had confirmation. Should I ring them again or will they think I'm a pain in the arse? No, I'll leave it. I've sent it so they must have it, but then what if they don't? My first fixture and, if it goes wrong, I'll never live it down. In the end I decide not to ring them. I'm sure it will be okay.

I check my phone again. It's 8.15, the lads should be getting on the bus now. If it hasn't turned up, I can expect a phone call. I stare at my phone, praying it doesn't ring. The minutes tick by ... 8.30 still no call, it must have turned up then. I breathe a sigh of relief.

I get picked up in Castleford. We arrive at the pub on time and, as I step off the team bus, I am praying that there is no problem with the food order or the booking. We go in and I introduce myself, check that everything is in place. The tables are set up, we are assured the order is being prepared and I breathe out again.

In the event, it all goes swimmingly. The players and staff are able to get on with their jobs and everyone is blissfully unaware that I am a nervous wreck for most of the day.

Never the Easy Option

EARLY FEBRUARY 2018

I always knew the worst part of this job would be breaking bad news to players. We fly to Australia in a few days to play Wigan in the first ever Super League game outside of Europe. Lee Radford has chosen the squad and it has fallen to me to inform one player that we won't be including him with us on the trip of a lifetime.

Originally, he'd been part of our plans, but having committed a second breach of discipline in a few weeks it wouldn't be fair to take him and leave a junior behind. He takes it badly, bursts into tears.

Later that day, I also have to inform Nick Rawsthorne that we will be letting him go for the rest of the season. That one goes a bit better. I think he was expecting it, but it has still been a difficult day.

LATE FEBRUARY 2018

The trip to Australia is behind us now. Although we lost both games, it was great PR for the club and a good trip for me personally. I caught up with old mates but, more than anything, enjoyed being around players again when I hoped my presence brought value.

A few days after returning home, on my laptop, I'm missing that feeling as I submit dual-registration forms to the RFL for our players who are with Doncaster that weekend. Then I have to copy and paste the RFL-approved wording into their contracts. I know it needs to be done and is important but I'm not sure why it's me that's doing it.

Now, I'm no longer so sure what I bring to the club.

I'm sure it will change. At least I hope it will.

FRIDAY 15 MARCH 2018

A busy week. The football department is getting ready for Easter. I've completed my first contract negotiation and we've sold Liam Watts to Castleford. It started with Paul Hatton asking me if we can get a cryotherapy unit in for the weekend. I always loved anything that could give me an edge over my opponent, so I understand Hatto's thinking, but it will cost five grand!

I tell him that I'll speak to Adam, it's his money after all.

Next up is the deal I am putting together for Masi Matongo, a 19-year-old prop that we have brought through the ranks carefully over the last few years. His development has really accelerated of late to the point where he has overtaken his contract; by that I mean he is playing like a man on a boy's wages. He deserves a review.

I speak to Lee Radford and CEO James Clark. We come up with a figure that we feel reflects his new value to the squad. Masi and his agent are happy with it and the deal is done in no time at all. It feels like a good day's work. I'm pleased with playing my part in moving things on so smoothly. Negotiations won't all be that easy though. Masi is a player we want to keep. I know there'll be blokes we won't and the prospect of that conversation is already eating away at me.

Liam was sold a week-and-a-half after being sent off for the fourth time in a year, a pantomime headbutt on Warrington's Dom Crosby the reason, on Sky TV. It was a ludicrous incident but typical of Wattsy at that point in his career, as was his response in the days that followed. It was too much for the head coach and the upshot of it was his departure. I had no role to play in that other than to encourage Scott Taylor to take a greater leadership role in the days and weeks that followed.

But Liam's departure throws longer-term recruitment planning into disarray. Taking over from Motu, I inherited his spreadsheet which showed our playing roster and the length and size of each contract in the current year, as well as in future ones. It is like a giant jigsaw puzzle and there are lots of considerations to make.

In 2018, a number of senior players were coming towards the end of their careers and we either needed to identify a junior that could come through and replace them, or we had to bring someone in from elsewhere. That was already scheduled, but now that Watts has left it leaves another void which will no doubt change our plans.

It is a fascinating aspect of my new role and has given me a real insight into how clubs have to operate in a salary-capped sport. In 2019, there was some dismay among supporters when one of our highly regarded local players left the club. He had come through the ranks and played quite a bit of Super League, but had still not really established himself regularly in the side. With his contract up for renewal, he asked for a big increase in salary. In the event, the club felt that he wasn't worth it and he took his services elsewhere. It's all well and good getting yourself a big contract but it's not going to do you any good in the long run if you can't perform at that level.

WEDNESDAY 24 APRIL 2018

It is the week before the Catalans away game and a bit busier than normal. At the moment, I'm preparing for the team to fly to France, putting together the manifest for the equipment we're taking and organising the bus to pick us up at the airport.

I'm looking forward to this trip as spending time amongst the playing group is where I feel most comfortable and where I have something to offer. It's been around five months since I started this job now and I cling to these opportunities and any other chance I get to speak to the players, especially the younger ones. Such as when James Clark asked me to have a chat with Lewis Bienek, show him around the training ground and try to persuade him to sign for us. In the event, I spent most of the day with him.

Lewis came to the club's attention as a 19-year-old, playing for London. At the time, he was already on Wigan's radar and there was talk of one or two clubs in the NRL sniffing around. Like many people, I had seen the highlights video on YouTube and knew that he had a huge amount of potential. It was clear that he had to leave London and move north if he was going to be successful and so the next move for him was a huge one.

I was reminded of the effort put in by people at Wests Tigers to convince me to sign. I had been given a very slick and professional presentation by the folks at Manly but ultimately it was the openness and atmosphere there that swung it. Just like Manly had with me, I knew that Wigan had given Lewis a very impressive overview hoping to tempt him, so I appreciated that I had my work cut out.

We talked about the club and the values that attracted me to sign for them, the supporters, the passion and how the city is absolutely nuts for rugby league. I took him to the stadium, the training ground and talked to him about a few of the areas where he might want to live. Gradually, I tried to sell the club to him without being too pushy. 'It's a big decision,' I told him. 'You should take advice from as many people as possible, but ultimately it has to be one that you're happy with because, once it's made, all the people giving you advice will fade into the background and it will be you who is left to make it work.'

In the end, he chose Hull and, for once, I felt like I had done something worthwhile.

TUESDAY 3 JULY 2018

We've been knocked out of the Challenge Cup, we are going nowhere in the league and injuries are no better. It's a tough place to be at the minute and my own job satisfaction isn't great either. I need a break.

Thankfully I am about to get one, although this is no holiday as I am due to set off on the 'Race Across Europe' cycling challenge in support of the Steve Prescott Foundation, along with my fellow ex-league players Ewan Dowes, Steve Hall and Steve Hampson, plus Darren Harrison, Phil Ellison, Kev Humphries and Steve Prescott's brother, Neil.

When I first signed up with the team, I had little idea what it was all about. It was a great way for me to get some exercise and have something to challenge myself with, even though it cost me two grand for a new bike! It was only when I began to study the route and look at the logistics involved that I realised the scale of it.

It would be a three thousand-mile journey through France, Germany and Austria before heading south into Italy and Slovenia. We were then scheduled to track west back to Italy through the Alps and back into France before crossing the Pyrenees to Spain. The route flattened out as we headed south, finally finishing in Gibraltar.

The record for an eight-man team was seven and a bit days. To beat it we had to be on the road non-stop, splitting into two teams with each one on the road for eight hours while the other guys rested. Every rider was to cycle pretty much flat out for twenty minutes before handing over to the next.

The arrangements were extremely complicated to ensure that all the riders and their bikes were in exactly the right place at the right time. It didn't always go smoothly but, after a few days, we seemed to iron things out and made good progress.

The biggest challenge was lack of sleep. We were on the road constantly and the best we could do was try and catch an hour here and there as we rolled around in the back of the support vehicles. But the discomfort was worth it once adrenalin kicked in and the camaraderie and views more than made up for the inconvenience.

Altogether I had around fifty stints on the bike and might have managed twenty hours sleep in total. I loved every minute. Taking on a fifteen per cent hill climb in the Alps in the dead of night with only the headlamps of the support vehicle to light the way is something I will never forget. And it was an incredible atmosphere as we arrived in Gibraltar in the early hours of the morning, having completed the route in six days, nineteen hours and seven minutes, smashing the previous record.

The whole adventure had been an amazing experience.

Before we set off, I had been meeting up with the rest of the team a couple of times each week and, as it bonded and my own cycling ability improved, I gained huge pleasure from being part of a group once again. Although we were meant to be doing our bit for a good cause, I can't thank the SPF charity, my fellow riders and the twenty plus support team enough for what they gave for me at that time.

MID-JULY 2018

I am at work again and down to earth with a bump. The Alps and Gibraltar seem a long way away and I am fed up. Without the day-in, day-out grind of training, preparing, playing and figuring out how I can keep getting better, I don't know what to do with myself.

The team are struggling on the field and the atmosphere around the whole club has become sour after massive defeats to Wakefield and Warrington. We've got six or seven of our most experienced players sidelined for the season, four or five others turning out with injuries, and the youngsters are playing far too many games than is good for them. They're trying their best to get up for each remaining fixture, but the season cannot end soon enough.

In the midst of all this, I can't do anything to help. I have always prided myself on giving my all for every club I have worked at, never letting anyone down, but in my current role there is nothing I can do to make things better.

My phone rings one night and it is Adam Pearson. Things are about to look up. 'I don't think I'm the right man for this job,' I tell him. 'You're not getting the best out of me.' I was pretty forthright and pleased to hear that he agreed with my assessment.

'Radders is looking for some help with the coaching,' he told me. 'Why don't you speak to him and try to sort something out?'

We had a rule at Hull that you weren't allowed to use your mobile in the physio's room. It is a place to be taken seriously, you have to listen to what you're told and avoid distractions, so no phones. It made sense, except nobody really paid any attention.

They did at first, but once one of the lads pulled their phone out of their pocket and started tapping and got away with it, everybody else followed suit. During 2016, when we were winning every week, everyone had their phones out and no one seemed to mind. When we lost a few games, there would be a bit of a clampdown, but it was never a rule that was applied consistently.

In all successful cultures, there must be a set of standards that everyone follows and an understanding that they will be consistently applied. If players don't believe that the coach means what he says, or it's for no reason other than to raise a bit of fine money for the team kitty, then his credibility and rules themselves are diminished. To ignore them challenges the authority of the coaching staff and the ethic of the entire group. I've never believed in anything as much as I do that.

Players need certainty, like kids, clear and consistent boundaries. If there is non-conformity, everything from the time training starts to how many sets to do in the gym, to how to prepare the night before a game... it all starts to crumble.

We had always spoken about culture at Hull ever since I arrived in 2012. Proof of a winning one is how you deal with the highs and lows. In 2016, after the cup win, our season fell away. True, we celebrated big-style – most teams do – but there was more to it than that. The success we enjoyed, and again in 2017, was because we had a good team, decent players who battled for each other and a free-wheeling culture that was driven by the personalities of people like Frank Pritchard and Leon Pryce. We didn't worry too much about our shortcomings and it was a pleasure to go to training every day.

That's not to say we didn't work incredibly hard. We wouldn't have achieved anything if we hadn't. It just lacked the detail and structure for it to be sustainable over a long period of time.

Once standards are established and agreed, you can then recruit, train and mould your players to fit them, and it has to be everyone at the club from the scholarship, academy and first team to the front office – they all have to buy into those expectations of each other all of the time. But it's hard, which is why only the best clubs achieve it.

What we struggled to eradicate was what I would call the 'banter' culture at Hull. It had existed for as long as I had been at the club, not just taking the piss out of each other but, more worryingly, out of the values you pretend to uphold. At the top clubs, they know when the banter ends and the serious stuff begins.

I was captain for most of Lee Radford's reign as coach and so accept my share of responsibility. I wasn't really one to call people out and would rather lead by example, but that probably wasn't much help to the coaching staff. One of my biggest regrets was an incident that occurred during our trip to Australia in 2018. If you asked most of the boys they wouldn't have remembered it, but it has played on my mind ever since. I'd just started my new role as football manager, but still felt responsibility for how everyone behaved.

By then, Liam Watts had been involved in a few misdemeanours which had become an issue for the coaching staff and team. We were all at dinner one night and he took it upon himself to stand up in front of everyone to say a few words. I could tell from his manner and his first couple of sentences that he was readying himself for a heartfelt apology. But he got no further than that when one of the players shouted: 'Shut up and sit down,' which led to an outburst of laughter from the entire room. I was sitting next to Wattsy and I could see that this was a genuine attempt to rebuild a few bridges so I attempted to shush the crowd in order to let him speak, but it fell on deaf ears and he returned to his seat.

Here was an opportunity for me to take a stand. I wasn't strong enough in that moment to allow Wattsy to say his piece and it was gone. I don't know whether things might have turned out differently, and his ultimate move to Castleford was probably the change that he needed anyway, but there was an opportunity that night to tackle something bigger. It pained me that we had still not yet fully developed a sustained high-performance culture at the club. I know it's not easy, but it is achievable with patience and the right approach and with Tony Smith now at the helm it can get there.

A few weeks after I came home from Melbourne, I was back at Hull's training ground. Josh Bowden was returning from injury, but struggling. He went for a run and broke down after just a few steps. I walked over, sat down next to him and we talked. He was really upset, close to tears, telling me how hard he found it. I mentioned the injuries I'd had and how difficult it had been to return, but that ultimately all the sacrifice and perseverance was worth it. I tried to reassure him that he would come through it. A little later, assistant coach Andy Last said to me: 'Nobody at this club has ever taken that much time to talk to Josh or any other injured player, come to think of it. You'll never realise how important that was for him coming from someone like yourself.'

When we met up, Lee Radford asked me what I could bring to the coaching team. It was a good question. I had already spoken about my reservations about becoming a coach. I always believed that there were those players who were destined to be and others, like me, that weren't. Coaches saw rugby league like a game of chess; I just saw blokes running at each other. In previous conversations with Andy Last when he had discussed the subject and I mentioned to him that I didn't see the subtleties he did, he told me that I spotted things like the willingness in players, outcomes of personal battles and attitude that he didn't.

It was an enlightening chat which helped me answer the question Radders had put to me. It was also around this time that I travelled to Melbourne to study their footballing department which reignited my passion for the game and reassured me that I had something to offer through coaching.

I'd sorted out my level 2 coaching badge and we agreed on the role I would take. With a few games left of what had become a disastrous season, Radders gave me a chance to see what I could do. 'Can you do the video session for the forwards before the Wigan game?' he asked, posing me just the kind of challenge I relished.

In the next few days, I spent hours with our analyst, Richard Peaks, as he showed me how to cut pieces of video together. Then even more time choosing the clips and preparing my presentation. I took it very seriously and was very nervous at the prospect of standing in front of the players and talking to them as a coach.

For me, 2018 was a difficult year. Rachael later suggested that there were times when she thought I showed signs of depression. She might be right. I spent a lot of the time trying to put a positive spin on how it was going, but deep down I wasn't happy and I found it difficult to discuss how I felt. Nowadays, we hear a lot about men's mental health and, in rugby league, we have got better at creating an environment where players, and more particularly ex-players, can discuss how they're feeling, but I still found it difficult.

On the face of it, I had everything I could dream of. I'd had a hugely successful playing career which I had the good fortune to end on my own terms, a loving and supportive family and, although not financially secure, I wasn't broke either. And, unlike lots of ex-players, I had been handed a great opportunity with a new job that kept me in the game. Nevertheless, I'd still lost my sense of purpose in life and found myself slowly sinking into a hole. Your reality is your own and only you can have that perspective about it.

I also spoke to Chris Rostron of Rugby League Cares, while participating in the next 'Ride to Wembley' charity bike effort. He explained that my scenario was exactly the kind that the charity needed to break down in order to help players to open up without judgment. He listened to me and it helped keep me sane. I had read stories about people going off the rails after they'd stopped playing and never remotely thought it could happen to me, but it did.

There were times that year when I wished I had a proper trade so I could just go and get a normal job and not have to worry about trying to find a new career in rugby. But, apart from stacking shelves in Somerfield when I was eighteen, I had never done anything else.

I began to think deeply about my life and feared my best years were behind me. I felt fortunate to have had such amazing playing experiences, but there was also regret that I couldn't do it anymore.

21

Not Quite the Final Curtain

EARLY JANUARY 2019. A THURSDAY night at Hull's training ground. It has been a long day. Having helped out with first team training in the morning, I'd stayed around preparing for the reserve team session I'd be running.

Kirk Yeaman, John McCracken and Richard Tate are alongside me to assist with the coaching but, mostly, to help me put a team together. John has great connections in the community game, while Rich coaches the England students. We end up with twelve 'terms and conditions' players, plus a few members of the first team squad to work with. I have them for two hours every Thursday night, hoping to whip them into a side that will play a dozen or so games in some form of reserves competition.

Over previous days, I have prepared a session which I hope will challenge their skills and stamina. Confidently, for once, I stand before them and explain the first drill. What follows is chaos. Instead of the tight, regimented exercise I'd imagined in my head, there were blokes running in all directions. One was jogging, another sprinting flat out. One kept the ball in hand, another had passed it to his mate, someone else hadn't picked a ball up, but set off running anyway.

They didn't have a clue what to do and hadn't understood me at all but, to their credit, didn't want to let me down. They were doing whatever came to mind. After a stray ball hit me on the head, I called a halt to proceedings and had a go at explaining the next drill. This time I did it more slowly, simplifying it, remembering that most of those listening as intently as they could were part-timers, not NRL players. It was a learning curve for me as much as them.

When it came to coaching, I knew I had to start at the bottom and was happy to do so. As well as looking after the reserves, I became the fourth (and very much junior) member of the first team coaching staff with a remit to work with the forwards, a role I soon relished.

Masi Matongo was the first person I'd signed as football manager, and I really liked him. He came to the game relatively late and, as well as being blessed with an ideal frame for a prop, he is one of the nicest lads I've met. I hoped I might be able to teach him a few tricks and spoke to him a lot during that pre-season. I talked to him about making his battles personal, preparation before the game, putting in those extra few hours on the weights, trying to visualise himself getting stronger.

Masi caught a big blow from Hull KR prop Mose Masoe in the pre-season derby. He shrugged it off and got on with his game which pleased me no end. Later he got in a similar hit on his rival, knocking him off his feet, showing a real intent to make his mark. He hadn't forgotten what we'd discussed. I was standing on the touchline at the time, bottle of water in hand, and couldn't resist racing onto the pitch to congratulate him on putting into practice all we'd discussed. After another game he was disappointed with his performance and felt he hadn't carried the ball enough. I told him that happens and to find other ways to make a contribution instead, like putting some energy into a kick chase or being aggressive from marker. In those few weeks in early 2019, I still felt like I was playing, but through Masi.

It was similar the following season when I spent time with Jack Brown, another promising forward. I spoke to him about training and getting the most possible out of every session, even if you don't feel like it, physically or mentally. I told him that I often hated it, which surprised him, but that I always found a purpose to do it with the most intensity I could.

The time I spent around the players was building my confidence and being part of the first team support also gave me a voice, which I used to try and bring about a few things I'd seen in Melbourne, like more regular staff meetings. Good communication between coaches and backroom staff is crucial in any sports team and I was pleased when Lee Radford adopted my suggestion.

I'd desperately missed playing; more than I could ever imagine. Coaching brought a sense of purpose and I began to think about the satisfaction and pleasure I'd get if I could help a group of players to enjoy the same kind of success I'd had. I began my coaching journey with very modest ambitions and, although I am confident enough that I have something to offer as part of a team, I still doubt I could be a head coach. In my experience of working for some great ones, they all have one thing in common: an ability to put the interests of the team above those of any individual and most definitely above their own relationships with players and staff. Although I care less and less about what people think of me as I grow older, I'm not sure I could handle all the tough conversations.

I could never be a 'hairdryer' type, that's not my style. I would rely on the consistency I see best in Tony Smith, where his relentless approach to day-to-day routines and standards of behaviour means he very rarely has to confront anyone. His players do it for him, because his standards become those of the group.

After a poor start in 2019, with Chris Green and Josh Bowden out injured, Scott Taylor suspended and Mickey Paea struggling with his form, Lee asked if I fancied coming out of retirement for a few weeks. It hadn't been the first time. A year earlier, after a chaotic cup game against Featherstone when we finished with nine on the field, he'd suggested I dig my boots out. I had actually gone to the trouble of resuming training but decided, at the last moment, that I didn't want to be responsible for denying a junior player their opportunity.

This was different. A downturn in mood during 2018 convinced me that I had retired too early. Although my new coaching role had brought a renewed sense of purpose, it was only because I was closer to the action. After thirteen straight defeats, including the season before, there weren't any candidates I'd be taking a place from. Perhaps I could bring more to the team if I took the field alongside them. There was always a risk it could end badly with injury from being out for so long or, worse, if I couldn't hack it. But I was excited at the prospect, much more than I had been during my 'last' season.

We lined up a reserve game against Wakefield. I found myself the centre of attention at Bishop Burton that Saturday afternoon but did a decent stint. More importantly, given the situation Hull were in, I felt that my presence in the middle brought out a bit of extra effort and energy from those around me. It all became a bit embarrassing at the end of the game, when some Wakefield players asked to have a selfie taken with me, but overall I was pleased with how it went. Physically, I came through it okay in the following days.

Without making any grand announcement, I was named in a 19-man squad for a Super League game with Wigan. On the Thursday before, we'd decided I was definitely going to play. I had stepped up training and, although I knew that a few days of extra weights and conditioning could never replace a full pre-season schedule, I wasn't too worried about my state of fitness. I anticipated it would be tough, but was more relaxed about a game than I had been in years.

I started on the bench and, as planned, went on after twenty-five minutes. As much as I'd looked forward to it, it was still an extremely unpleasant experience. On my first carry, I drove in at Sam Powell, who got himself underneath me and dropped me face first into the DW pitch. At least it earned us a penalty. A few minutes later, I was the third man into a tackle and Danny Houghton's head collided with my ear. It was ringing for the rest of the game, black for a week. And then one of their young lads ran at me and I ended up with a stinger at the top of my shoulder. The pain was shooting down my arm and I couldn't straighten it.

Just before half-time, we found ourselves endlessly defending. It was relentless. I was exhausted, the trainer came on to check how I was, but I brushed him away. When the hooter went, I'd never been more pleased to go in at half-time. I'd played for just fifteen minutes.

I did another twenty straight after the break. My timing was a bit off and some of my agility was missing, but I made good contacts and, on one occasion, put in a really big hit on one of their forwards. My teammates rushed in to give me a slap on the back. There's nothing like that feeling, I had forgotten how much I had missed it.

Nobody expected us to win, the pressure was all on them. I could see we were enjoying it and was pleased to have brought something to the team that had been lacking. We rode our luck in the second half, it went to golden-point extra-time, and thankfully we had Mark Sneyd, who nailed the drop-goal to win us the game. After digging in so well I'm not sure what it would have done to us psychologically if we had lost. We would have been broken and it might have set us back a while, effectively killing our season before it really began.

In the weeks after my return, I saw the difference in the squad. They were more upbeat and seemed to bring more energy to their game; it was hugely satisfying, however hard. I went home each day more content than I had been in years. I couldn't put my finger on it, but it felt good. Now the senior citizen of Super League, I played the following week and the week after that. After a while, Radders asked if I would play on for the rest of the season and I said I would. It helped that I wasn't killing myself in training. Paul Hatton was crucial to that, he really looked after me. We are all carefully tracked in training anyway and it has been that way for years, wearing GPS gear under our training kit, which monitors everything.

Things were going so well from a personal point of view that it wasn't long before I was asked if I might even go around again, do another pre-season, and play in 2020. I had been giving it some thought. I'd be 39 soon after the season started, but didn't feel that old and it been done before. Aussie great Steve Menzies was very nearly 40 when he finally packed it in and I have always kept myself in very good shape.

The biggest challenge was mental but, having resigned myself to playing 40-50 minutes per game and not every week, I felt I could keep going. Plus I'd also benefited from a year off. Sorting out a deal wasn't as straightforward as I hoped, however. I'd like to think I built up a good relationship with the hierarchy at Hull over the years and decided to speak to the club directly about my contract, nevertheless,

I was decidedly unimpressed with their first offer. Having spent 2018 as football manager, I knew what everyone else was earning and what I believed I was worth.

I did briefly flirt with the idea of going somewhere else for a year, but thankfully the club came back with another offer and I was happy to shake hands on it. Once again, I was pleased that they didn't overdo the publicity and kept it low key.

The team were woefully inconsistent during 2019. We just weren't strong enough mentally. We would find ourselves in tight games but lose our concentration, make an error, put ourselves under pressure and then crumble. On the Sunday night after Magic Weekend, I was sitting at home in front of the TV, a bit sore and fed-up. We had embarrassed ourselves the day before, shipping fifty points against Huddersfield in front of the rest of Super League, but I began to realise why I'd been enjoying my rugby so much, why I was weirdly content with my own performances. I felt little responsibility, which led to me playing with freedom. I knew that part of the reason why the club wanted to retain me was for my leadership and experience, but that pressure of always having to be at my best every day, afraid of doing or saying anything that might have a negative influence on other players, caused me to quit in 2017.

Throughout my career, that's what I did – pressured myself to get better every week, every day, every session. As soon as a game was won, I barely celebrated. If we'd lost, I would start the groundwork for the following week almost immediately. I was trapped in this cycle of hard work and worrying what might happen if I didn't prepare properly. I got my rewards with medals and caps but, once the injuries started, it became more and more demanding and exhausting. By 2017, I couldn't keep doing it, I'd had enough.

But, when I started playing again, I felt none of that. I wanted to do well and be influential, but I just did what I could. I realised that all of those things that I thought were expected of me, weren't.

What I was doing was enough.

22

Shutdown

ON 2 FEBRUARY 2020, I began my twenty-first professional rugby league season. It was twenty years and five months since I had made my debut in 1999, and it meant that I became one of only a handful of sportsmen to have played in four different decades.

My goals were modest – get through the season in one piece and enjoy it. If I could bring something to the group so much the better and, in the unlikely event that we won something, well what a way to finally go out.

We couldn't have started better, with comfortable wins against Leeds and Hull KR in front of full houses at Headingley and the KCOM. But it only took a few weeks for the usual frailties to re-emerge and, by March, Lee Radford was once again under pressure.

We surrendered a healthy lead at home to Catalans and it seemed only a matter of time before a change would be made. I played in that game and was expecting to sit out the one against Wakefield five days later, but sensing that defeat to Trinity might be the nail in the coffin for Radders I told him I wanted to play. We'd been through a lot together and I wanted to help if I could. We won narrowly but afterwards I was really struggling.

With each week that passed, my recovery was taking longer, however this time my knee was really bad. I feared I might not make it through the season.

The following week we lost heavily at home to Warrington. I watched from the stands as we folded badly in the second half and saw disgruntled supporters leave early, muttering. After the game, the dressing room was sombre. I was in there but didn't say anything. After a while, Lee came in and just said: 'That's it.'

We knew what he meant. While Adam Pearson broke the news live on Sky, Lee shared his feelings and thoughts with the players. He couldn't have handled it better. I felt relieved for him, it had become inevitable. In the aftermath, Adam took some stick for his handling of it, but the truth is that he spoke privately to Lee to give him the news before he went on TV to announce it.

It didn't take long for my name to be mentioned as a possible replacement, but I made it clear straight away that it wasn't going to be me. Even to consider myself suitable for the job would have been delusional and selfish. I didn't have what it would take, the man-management skills required to hold the group to account. Adam asked Andy Last to take over the reins while he began his search for a new head coach, saying he would take his time to get the right appointment.

But then suddenly, time was something we all had plenty of.

Like everyone, I watched with concern as the coronavirus started to spread from China to Iran to Italy and then the UK. I assumed it would fizzle out, but when they started to cancel football matches it dawned on all of us that this might be bigger than we imagined. Things were changing fast. Initially, we were told that we couldn't all train together and were given a slot when we could come into the training ground in groups of six. But that only lasted a day or so before the season was suspended and we were stood down entirely.

By the middle of that week, everything was closing, including our local gym, so I was forced into the garage to dig out an old rowing machine that had been gathering dust. At that stage, they had said we could be doing this until June and that seemed a long way away. Our conditioner and head of performance, Paul Hatton, set everyone up with their own personal training programme. Running was easy. The tracks and trails near us were understandably quiet and I could cycle for as long and as far as I wanted, but the weights sessions were a difficult thing to replicate. I got hold of some resistance bands and modified the kids' climbing frame to create something I could use. I'd do a couple of hours a day on that.

At home, things changed massively once the schools closed and the realities of lockdown kicked in. At first, Rachael was still at work – she had just started a new job – so I found myself looking after three kids. I tried to keep a routine. I would still get my gear out the night before, so I could go out prior to Rachael and the kids getting up. It wasn't always easy and there were some days when I really couldn't be bothered, but then Hatto started sharing all of our training times on WhatsApp and the competitive spirit kicked. I didn't dare miss a session.

The day continued with a Joe Wicks PE lesson in front of the TV, followed by attempts to home school Isaac and Eva, while Florence and our new puppy also competed for attention. It wasn't great. Ofsted would definitely have judged the Gareth Ellis Academy 'required improvement'. The minute Rachael stepped back through the door I would go out on my bike. An hour – and thirty miles or so – later, I'd come home refreshed and start writing lists. Like everyone at first, I saw lockdown as a great opportunity to get all of those little jobs done around the house, but when you've got an indeterminate amount of time to fill, there never seemed much urgency.

I'd heard about the furlough scheme, but wasn't really sure what it meant. We got an email from James Clark informing us that the club intended to apply for it. Without some support there was little chance that they could survive a prolonged closure. Hull outlined their offer to the players. The highest earners would take a pay cut of thirty-five per cent, while others would lose thirty and twenty. Those on the lowest wages – generally the young lads – wouldn't have their pay cut at all, and our wages would be underwritten by the furlough scheme.

Everyone accepted it. We didn't feel that we had much choice to be honest. If the club went bust – and Adam made it clear that was a real possibility – then we wouldn't have any contract at all. Plus, we could see what was happening everywhere else; people were losing their jobs, their businesses, their lives. I was just thankful that we were safe and healthy. Adam assured us that once we were able to return he would pay our contracts in full. That promise would come back to bite him on the arse, but at that time most of the squad felt as reassured and content as we could be with a global pandemic raging around us.

Through April and May I slipped into a routine unlike anything I'd ever experienced. I hadn't had so much prolonged rest for a long time and my general fitness grew with each passing week. My runs got longer, faster and more enjoyable. I would set out to do 10k and, thriving with the sensation of running pain-free, found myself clocking up sixteen or seventeen kilometres instead. Physically, I was in great shape. Mentally, I was quite relaxed as well and once we were told that the season was going to re-start, I really began to look forward to it. We were informed that we could return to training in July and begin playing again in August. The prospect of getting stuck into a shortened season of maybe a dozen more games, after such a long break, was really motivating.

Discussions about safety and logistics had been taking place amongst the owners and broadcasters and then the players became involved, through the GMB union. Rugby league players in England are woefully represented in the running of the game and have been for years. Various attempts have been made to organise them into a coherent unit capable of expressing a voice, but they have almost always failed. The game's administrators and club owners bear much of the responsibility for ignoring players' views for decades, but the players themselves have to cop some blame for their reluctance to join the GMB. The union needs 80 per cent of the professional players signed up before they can demand formal recognition and they have always been a long way from that.

In recent years, Geoff Burrow – Rob's dad – and Garreth Carvell have become the voice of the players in negotiations with the RFL and club owners. Throughout the Covid crisis and lockdown, they really stepped up, which led to a surge in membership. Scott Taylor was the Hull player representative in those meetings and he kept us informed about the talks taking place. We knew about the timescale, playing behind closed doors and the proposed 'six again' rule, it all made sense.

The biggest wrangle, unsurprisingly, was around wages as most owners were desperate to cut their wage bills. Adam had promised that we would be paid our contracts in full once we returned to training but when it came down to it he had to admit that he couldn't honour that and we all had to take a fifteen per cent cut. Even that was much better than what was on offer at most clubs and the disparities led to a hold up before the season could begin again. With just three weeks before fixtures were set to resume, there were still only three clubs signed up.

In the event, deals were done that ensured everyone could go back to training and playing and, if there was something positive to come out of the whole situation, perhaps it is in the strengthened voice of the players. For years, they have always just rolled over and accepted any changes, whether it be in terms of the salary cap, the schedule of the season or the rules of the game.

I put it down to the culture of rugby league, which is ironically also one of our strengths. We are a pretty stoic group, we just get on with it, but that can also be very damaging. We don't ask enough questions and that has led to the situation where players do not feel that they have an avenue or right to be heard.

What impressed me during those weeks was the way in which players put aside their club loyalties and supported one another. I became part of many WhatsApp groups involving those from other clubs. Rather than being divided by the owners, we came together as one group to make it clear it wasn't right, for example, that Wigan should throw money at new signings while simultaneously trying to cut the wages of players and other staff. I heard lots of intelligent opinions from players and perhaps a willingness to use it, not least around the perennially thorny question of fewer games, which would ultimately lead to a better spectacle.

Everything about the lifting of lockdown was a trade-off. If we wanted to be completely safe, we wouldn't be playing or training at all and isolating instead. But if we wanted to keep our livelihoods and help the sport survive, we had to find a way back. There were lots of changes and necessary safety measures that started before we left home. I got up, took my temperature and sent it, along with answers to a short questionnaire checking whether I had any virus symptoms, in to the club. Once I reached the training ground I'd be temperature checked again and asked again if I had any symptoms, all the while tracking a one-way route around the training facility. It felt odd, but importantly it also felt safe.

We trained in groups of six, doing our preparation together, splitting into pairs to do our weights, then back into our mini group for some work on the field. Only on Tuesdays, Thursdays and Saturdays did we come together as a full team, doing some contact and working on calls. And then, when we were finished, we would leave just as we arrived, still in our training gear, going straight home for a shower.

Each Monday, we were tested for Covid at the training ground. It was a necessity, although quite unpleasant experience, and we would usually find out the result the following day. It struck me from the outset that being tested just once a week didn't seem like enough and it was a question raised with the RFL. But their doctor seemed confident that it was fine and the discussion didn't get any further than that. It would only be a few weeks before that particular decision would be called into question.

Until 2020, the closest I had ever come to playing a game behind closed doors was in my early days at Wakefield. We travelled to Chorley for a cup game against Lancashire Lynx and there were about 600 fans there; you could hear individual conversations taking place in the crowd. Arriving at Headingley for our first game during lockdown had the same eerie feeling. Salford were our opponents and ours was the first of a triple-header. There really was nobody there when we pulled up, not even anyone from the other teams.

For four weeks, we had trained well, working hard in every session and ripping into each other when allowed, but the mood had been odd during the captain's run. It was quieter than normal, the banter had disappeared and, when a few errors crept in, the lads seemed tetchy with each other. I spoke about it afterwards.

Salford's season, like ours prior to shutdown, had been indifferent so it was likely to be a finely balanced game. However, in the quiet, we lost 54-18. I questioned myself and spoke to Lasty and Danny Houghton about whether I could still make a contribution. They said I did, but in my regular column in the *Yorkshire Post* I publicly said we had a soft underbelly. The article came out on the Monday after the Salford game and I was prepared for a few comments when I turned up for training that day, but no one said a word.

As normal, I had my Covid test, did my group work, and an extended session alongside Danny. Tuesday was a day off. We had been out all day and I hadn't really looked at my phone, but as I packed my training bag that night I noticed I had a message. It was a text from Andy Last, a long one. After reading the first few lines, the shock hit me.

Six of our players, plus two members of staff, had tested positive for Covid. We were to stay away from the training ground with immediate effect until we had more information. At that time, I still felt quite cut off from the disease. I genuinely didn't know anyone that had been struck down by the virus. The message didn't say who was affected, but it only took a few minutes for our WhatsApp group to cough up the news. Those that had it were quick to share, and keen to reassure everyone else, that they were fine and not showing any serious symptoms.

Danny was one who was positive. I then went into my own 'track and trace' mode. I had spent most of the day with him and then gone to see my sixty-eight-year-old dad. Panic started to build. I called dad and told him the news, which hadn't broken yet. I tried to stay calm, but also be as honest as I could. There was no denying that I had inadvertently put him at risk and he needed to know what had happened, but nor did I want him to worry too much. He was calm. I told him that I was fine, had no symptoms, and would get in touch with him the next day.

The news broke and within a few hours, the blame game started. There was some speculation that a small group of players had mixed together socially after the game and that this gathering could have been responsible for the infection spreading. I had seen the picture of them on social media, sitting in a garden and I had cursed them for being so stupid. Why would you post a picture of yourselves on social media after a performance like that anyway? Whether they were at risk of spreading the virus or not, it was a dumb thing to do.

We now know that it could have come into the camp from anywhere. In the following weeks, every club in the competition was hit by positive cases and games were being cancelled every few days but, unfortunately, we were the first and it felt like a huge deal at the time and typical of the year we were having.

I felt so sorry for Andy Last. Being Hull FC coach was the job he had always dreamed of, but now it was turning into a nightmare as we were told to stand down from training and isolate at home for fourteen days. During that time there was a flurry of testing and, by the end of the week, twelve people at the club, including eight players and Andy himself, had all tested positive.

After the Salford game, Lasty resolved to make some changes. Although he had to wait an extra few weeks he was good to his word when the next game came around at the end of August, against Huddersfield. Brad Fash, Jordan Lane, Jack Brown and Joe Cator had demonstrated terrific attitudes and deserved their chance. I would have been more than happy to sit out the game, but he wanted me in amongst them and so I started in the front row.

Andy hadn't had much chance to make an impact, but I did notice the changes to our training routines and the way in which he expected the players to behave and the standards he demanded. We ground out a win and it was only one game, but it was a good start.

The Challenge Cup came around with a tie against Castleford in the silence of St Helens, as only a few grounds were operative. I would normally have left the field around the twenty-minute mark, but this time kept going. I'd plenty of energy and was really enjoying tearing into their forward pack and, in particular, a youngster called Jacques O'Neill, who threw an elbow my way. I didn't mind, I was actually relishing the duel and thought of myself in that same position, twenty years earlier, trying to make my mark in the game, taking no backward steps. Afterwards, I sent him a message on Twitter telling him that I'd enjoyed the battle and liked his attitude.

As Castleford threatened to come back at us in the second half, I went on for a second spell and helped us to close the game out for a really enjoyable win – our best of the season. We sang 'Old Faithful' with gusto in the dressing room, the last time I did that as a player.

I pulled up badly in the following days, couldn't train, and my knee didn't feel right at all. I've had knee problems for most of my career. It feels clunky, the joint clicks and grinds from time to time, sometimes it gets stuck and I have to massage it with my hands to get it moving again. It's like my upper and lower leg are not properly connected and something is stuck in between. I'd played with it for years, but now it was taking longer to settle down. The team run to face Wigan in the next round was on a Thursday and I took part, gingerly. I spoke to Lasty again at the end of the session and he could see my concern, but asked me for 25 minutes out there.

I walked back to my car, hobbling. Climbing in, I had to lift my leg up into the foot well and sat there staring out of the window. The following day, I was expected to throw myself into battle against a fearsome pack yet could barely walk, what was I doing? I also thought about young Jack Brown sitting at home, desperate to play in a Challenge Cup quarter-final while an old man on one leg was stopping him from doing so.

The next day, I watched from home as we were given a master-class by a tremendous Warriors side. My final game, appropriately, had been in the Cup against Castleford – the club I'd supported as a boy; it could not have been more fitting. Twenty-one years and one day since I had made my debut, I'd played my final game.

With no chance of winning anything, my motivation for playing again disappeared. The following week, I went to see our club doctor, Andrew Edwards, who also happens to be a knee specialist. Lasty came with me, mostly as a friend rather than my coach. I think he knew it was going to be a tough day for me and that I'd probably want someone to talk to afterwards. The doc told me I had arthritis in there and the bone had deteriorated to such an extent that there was not much left to work with. Steroid injections would numb the pain, but each one would only make it worse. He confirmed that at some point I'd need a knee replacement, but if I stopped playing it would settle down and might not be for a while yet.

That was all I needed to hear. There was nothing left to achieve, nothing to prove, but a great deal to lose. I spoke to Rachael and rang my dad, who completely agreed that this was the right decision. I put a message on our family WhatsApp group and my sisters and brothers-in-law all weighed in with the same sentiment.

I had already sent a text to Andy Last but waited a few days before I called James Clark. He didn't want the club to make any big announcement while the season was still going. He wanted me to stay around, supporting Lasty and the younger lads and, of course, I was happy to do that. In the weeks that followed, I enjoyed being a part of a team that was building a bit of momentum on the training ground and the pitch, getting a big win on our return to the KCOM Stadium as we hammered the Tigers.

With the virus creeping back into training grounds, more and more games were cancelled across the country, so the RFL decided to pull the plug on the season and jump straight into an expanded play-off series – and we were in it. I had signed for Hull in 2012, hopeful that I could leave the team in a stronger position. It wasn't easy and we were still way short of the standards set by St Helens and Wigan but, for the first time for many months, I felt optimistic.

In beating Warrington, we earned a semi-final against Wigan. Cheekily, a few people asked if I would play one more game if we made it to the Grand Final, which had been moved to our own KCOM Stadium. Anyone with a chance of playing in one would take it, but I knew deep down it wasn't going to happen. The group had earned their right to play every fixture now and, ultimately, it didn't matter anyway as the Warriors made it to the final freezing night.

I didn't want to make an announcement that I was retiring (I had done that once before) but the club persuaded me otherwise and so, not long after the Wigan game, they issued a short statement. What I didn't know was that they had also put together a video which they released at the same time. In it, lots of my teammates, opponents, friends and foes had been recorded, passing on their messages and tributes. When it was released, I was at Red Hall, home of the RFL, having a Covid test to allow me to attend the Grand Final. They had asked me to walk the trophy out in the empty stadium for TV. I was honoured and humbled to be sharing the spotlight, in some small way, with James Graham and Sean O'Loughlin, both of whom would be playing in their final game that night. I waited until I got home, went into our bedroom and watched the video alone on my laptop.

I had started playing rugby league with just one goal in mind, to earn the respect of my teammates and opponents. That was enough to drive me on for twenty years and, as I watched through teary eyes, it dawned on me that I had.

Shortly afterwards, the club also announced that they would be looking for a new head coach. Andy Last had, in my view, done a great job in difficult circumstances. He had steered the club through the whole lockdown period and the Covid outbreak and, despite that, had got to within 80 minutes of a Grand Final.

I would have loved to see him get the job on a permanent basis, but I think Adam had made his mind up early that he wanted to go in a different direction and Brett Hodgson was soon announced as Hull's new boss. I had come across Brett a few times over the years and knew him to be a highly competent and passionate man who was very highly-rated in the game.

23

Wheel Turns Full Circle

I FIRST HEARD OF BRETT HODGSON's reputation as soon as I got to Wests Tigers. He arrived at Huddersfield – where he became Man of Steel – the same season I went the other way, so we crossed.

He was held in enormous regard at the Tigers, one of the catalysts that led to the 2005 Grand Final win, his form over that historic season sensational. They selected their all-time team the other year and he is in at fullback, such is the esteem with which he is held. The boys constantly referenced him when I got out there in their stories, and we'd opposed each other when I returned and he was then at Warrington. So, without really knowing him well, when he was appointed at Hull as head coach we already had a lot in common.

When Brett was in for the FC job, at the request of the club, I remember asking some of the old Wests Tigers boys who'd played with and under him – because he'd gone back to coach at the Tigers at the time – what he was like. The reports were all excellent. They said you could have a good laugh with him, but he was a very good technical coach and really knew the game, so it was an appointment that I looked forward to. That was all subject to him wanting me on his staff as an assistant, of course, by no means certain due to my association with the old, failed regime. But I did get a call asking me if I wanted to be his defensive coach, which I gladly took up.

What no Hull coach has had in recent times, probably going back to Albert Kelly, is a settled, regular dominant halfback, such a key, pivotal role to build a side around. Josh Reynolds wasn't a success. Jake Connor never really had a settled position. Luke Gale got off to a difficult start with a five-match ban from which he never really recovered. Even Jake Clifford, who came after them and was starting to make that impact, went back to North Queensland after a single season, just as he was finding his feet.

It's been something of a problem position for years. None of them had quite the impact of a Paul Cooke or Richard Horne or, talking of overseas players, Adam Dykes. In fact, I heard one of the fans say at a forum that Clifford was the best he'd seen in the role since Peter Sterling came over in the mid-1980s. Albert, as unorthodox as he was, left with reputation high after some unbelievable performances but he wasn't there long enough to make a mark, those following him even less so.

It just didn't work out for Josh Reynolds. It hadn't at Wests Tigers either, where he came from, despite him having had such a glittering career at Canterbury Bulldogs and with New South Wales. Some of that pressure of being the go-to man wore heavily on him at Hull, because I don't think he was the kind of player we all wanted him to be. He was very gritty and dogged and possibly thought that, with his NRL experience, coming into Super League might be easier, but it's a different style of competition. It's every bit as tough – there's always someone, whatever level you play, trying to knock your head off, especially if you are the supposed heartbeat of the side.

Jake Connor was very talented but completely different to Josh, who at least was trying hard but not quite producing the goods. Jake was, intermittently, coming up with them, but wasn't such a hard worker and that led to consistency issues. Brett, particularly at the start of his time, threw all his eggs into the Jake Connor basket. Knowing his ability, he felt that he could get him onside and mould the team around him, which would have been the perfect scenario. But he never did. Once the experiment began to fail, Brett jumped into picking Jake out in video sessions, which meant he got a bit shirty in return. Before he knew it, Brett had lost everybody. It got pretty toxic towards the end.

That's not a slight on him, more that he was an inexperienced head coach trying to find his way and it was a bigger job than he'd anticipated. It's not all about rugby in that role. It's managing people, emotions and different characters. The best coaches can do that, whether everyone likes each other or not. Somehow, they can bring a group together and there's a real skill to it.

In July 2001, because of Covid, I had to step in and take over the head coaching role with Keiron Purtill, as Brett had tested positive. By then I'd got a bit more of a feel for what was expected of me and started to do things my way. Being in charge was more fun than I'd imagined, even though it was daunting getting the remaining staff together to plan what was needed. I did some of the pre and post-match media too, which gave me more insight into the head coach's role – and we won 64-22, a one hundred per cent win record, which didn't look bad on my CV!

Controversy reigned when we were knocked out of the Challenge Cup at the semi-final stage by St Helens, after a key incident when Josh Griffin dropped the ball having snapped his Achilles tendon and Theo Fages picked it up to run in a try.

Many said it was unsportsmanlike and an injustice, but I could see it from both sides. As a kid, we were always told to never let go of the ball no matter what until the referee blows his whistle. It was a fundamental non-negotiable, akin to getting back into a defensive line even if your leg's broken. But having experienced such a rupture and the excruciating instant pain, I can perfectly understand why Josh would release it. In that split second, I would probably have done the same as Theo; his instinct was to play exactly what he saw without knowing any of the circumstances and, once he had, there was no going back.

It was a disappointing season all round as we also failed to make the play-offs. There was a concern, and again in the next one, that we'd set off well, picked up a lot of injuries and had both campaigns unravel from the midway point. That led to an examination of the pre-season schedule and how hard you should go, something that Tony Smith and Jason Davidson changed in 2023.

At the start of 2022, one of Hull's greatest ever players and coaches, Johnny Whiteley, passed away. It was a big reflective moment for the club and me. I'm a student of the game's history. To understand where you are, you need to know on who's shoulders you stand and Johnny was black and white through and through. He still went to the gym every day into his 90s; used to come into training and tell me tales of growing up on Hessle Road and working in the docks. We had some great chats, especially when I was the captain. He was brilliant at putting things into perspective no matter what the results, a welcome sounding board because he truly had seen and done it all.

As well as the multiple injuries that scuppered some of what Brett was trying to build, we also had issues with discipline, giving away too many penalties and picking up continual suspensions. That was partly down to the frustration felt by a number of players, not least the unsettled ones due to come off-contract. There wasn't a clear view of what the future held for them personally and the team going forward. The connections needed weren't there and it was often a case of every man for himself.

I still felt a bit on the outer. As someone who prided himself on trying to get the best out of myself and hopefully those around me, I began to question what I was doing again, whether I was good enough for the job. It wasn't a particularly enjoyable time.

I still didn't fully know what my role was. Keiron was effectively coaching the team from a technical point of view for a lot of the time and delivering session plans, something he had years of experience doing. He had a clear view of what needed achieving each day and I continued to learn a lot from him. I'd chip in around some of the areas I was responsible for but, being quite close to the players and having only recently come out of that environment, not to mention a decent judge of character with, I reckon, a high degree of emotional intelligence, I could see that it was all a bit of a mess. Players weren't on board, just waiting for the season to end, and that was being reflected in the results.

The worst was the penultimate game of the 2022 season, at home in the derby, when Rovers with fifteen men took us apart. It summed up the depths we'd sunk to by then and where everyone's head was. Unacceptably, the team just gave up in the most important fixture for the fans.

There was no way back for Brett after that and a good few players were waiting to see what happened to him before deciding on their own futures, especially the experienced guys like Scott Taylor and Danny Houghton. It was intensely disappointing for everyone and we looked like we were heading into the coming 2023 campaign on a downbeat note. Once more I started to question whether I was part of the problem rather than the solution.

Tony Smith coming in was a moment when I thought I'd give it one more crack. His appointment really excited me and I was offered a three-year deal under him. There had been more soul-searching during Brett Hodgson's reign at Hull as to whether I'd done the right thing going into coaching. It's fair to say that, with the players we had, we underachieved and that something within the group wasn't right and I did feel a certain responsibility for that. Under Tony, it felt more like a proper coaching apprenticeship. It was important to have that stimulus, where you come into work and learn every day. It brought back the times under him as a player between 2005-2007. Although he has changed and had mellowed a little, just a bit, there was still some of the old Tony there.

I was reminded that a number of the things I took from him and used throughout my career were still relevant regarding factors that make a good rugby player. That was quite heartening and reassuring. It took me back to some of the core principles of what made me as a player and I began to really enjoy it again. The theme going around the club was 'fresh start' and that included impressive new training facilities at the city's University, while Keiron and Paul Hatton were among those who moved on. That changed the ideas around what the pre-season regime should be and was just what the club needed.

Tony is so clear and concise when he delivers his messages. The players bought into his ideas and the way he wanted them to play, but it took time. After a decent start, Hull lost seven games on the trot, but Tony didn't panic. He was great during his reviews and engaged with every player, keen to hear their opinion and possibly even allow them to do it their way for a while until they came back to his. During the run of defeats, we were constantly correcting and gradually convincing more players to change their ingrained habits to how he saw it. It was a process that had to be gone through to get everyone on the same page.

A lot of Tony's philosophy is around team effort, digging in and not giving up for each other. As I write, that is starting to bear fruit.

24

Reflections

I'VE NEVER BEEN A GREAT one for hoarding things. Most of my medals and playing shirts, the ones I've kept, are in boxes in the loft or at my dad's house. I've still got my first Great Britain shirt, but I've given most of the others away. I've got a limited number I've swapped over the years – mostly for Australian or Kiwi ones, and there are a few French and Samoan jerseys in there as well. Usually from players I knew or opponents I really admired.

I've still got the one I wore in Sydney, in 2006, of course.

As for club shirts, I've kept those that really matter to me... the Wakefield one from my Super League bow in 1999 ... the Leeds colours I wore in two Grand Finals ... and my Wests Tigers debut. For each of Hull's Challenge Cup-winning finals in 2016 and 2017, we were given a second shirt to change into at half-time, which was ideal as I was able to give one away while keeping the other.

With regard to medals, my dad has got most of those as well, displayed in a cabinet – and mum deserves a mention as she is the one who cleans them! They look after them much better than I ever could. Dad has most of the other awards too. The individual ones are nice, but it is those I have won as part of a team that mean the most. It's the memories of being with your teammates and club staff that matter most as you reach the end of your career. When you celebrate, it's not so much about the silverware itself, it's everything you've done together to get there. That's why it is always so nice to meet up again and remember what you achieved. I'm lucky that I have had success at different clubs and in both hemispheres, and I will enjoy the reunion dinners until the end of my days.

I was a very physical player. I prided myself on dominating my opponent, but the game is altering. Towards the end of my playing career we outlawed the chicken-wing tackle, shoulder-charge, hip-drop. Soon, by the look of it, that list will include tackling height. I've gone through bemoaning that the sport might become more akin to touch and pass, to accepting that the world is changing and rugby league has to adapt with it. What I'm clear on is that it will always have that physical element of contact, the best players of every generation played it on the red line that existed at the time. If they went beyond it, they got sent off, which has happened since the sport was invented. The thresholds change and the challenge for the modern player now is to find their line; to discover how to still play it aggressively but within whatever the rules are. If any of my kids suddenly decided that they wanted to make a stab at the sport, I'd want those kinds of safeguards in place – and we desperately need to address participation at youth level.

Throughout my career, I have always found myself able to adapt my game to suit the level at which I was playing. I did it when I first broke into the Great Britain side and again moving to Australia. I put that down to the experience I had at Wakefield, moving rapidly from the academy team to the reserves and then to the first team.

I was awarded the player of the year trophy for three seasons on the trot when with Wests Tigers, a phenomenal accolade of which I'm immensely proud, but I genuinely don't think that I was the best player during my time there. I felt like I went and did my job. I was determined to put a marker down and establish a reputation because even though I was an international, I felt certain not too many NRL fans would know who I was. It had been a while since the last Englishman, Adrian Morley, had torn up the competition.

I could easily have been a flop, but that mantra of being the kind of player others wanted to have alongside them spurred me on and ultimately served me well. That appreciation was ultimately why I won such recognition.

Having to play at such a competitive level brought the best out of me and I probably played my finest rugby during those three seasons in Australia. The pressure to perform was immense. It was relentlessly tough and I nearly got sick of hearing Tim Sheens say: 'This is a must-win game' every week. One round, I'd be up against Nathan Hindmarsh; the next, Anthony Watmough. I was facing representative players every week and had to be on my mettle or else I'd have been made to look stupid.

I didn't always achieve the standard, but I tried my darndest. My level of consistency improved, always a seven or eight out of ten, and that's what got me the plaudits. There was never an occasion like at Leeds, when Rob Burrow and Danny McGuire would go out and destroy a side, where you would win by 40 points and cruise through the 80 minutes. My game changed in Australia as well. Part of that was playing off the likes of Benji Marshall, Rob Lui and Robbie Farrar, but also due to Tim Sheens bringing an extra dimension to it. I'd always seen myself as workmanlike, defence-orientated, a do-the-right-thing-for-the-team type of player, but he encouraged me to pass the ball as well, which no one else had.

Benji expected plenty too. If I wasn't where he needed me to be, he left me in no doubt. He demanded perfection so he would have multiple options open to him and I liked that. If I'm told what to do and where I need to be, I'll do it to the best of my ability. Again, that's probably what got me noticed over there and won their respect.

Tim played a really big part in adding that extra dimension to my play. Turn defensive sessions into attacking ones, that was his philosophy. He was very good for me and I've been very lucky throughout my career to get influential coaches at the right time.

John Harbin instilled mental toughness. Shane McNally started pushing me into a leadership role. Tony Smith, in terms of the technical side, really focused on the detail of the game. They all had a real impact on making me the player I became.

I tell any young player I come in contact with now – and some older ones who might take it for granted – that what we do as sportspeople, despite the sacrifices and injuries that can get you down, is a dream job. It's an honour that should be appreciated.

Few are as fortunate as me to be able to stop, have a break and then come back playing again. Taking such a sabbatical in 2018 reminded me of how much I missed playing and of what a great privilege it is to be paid to do something you love. In February 2020, I was reminded again of why I had returned when I met up with a bunch of teammates from my days at Leeds. We came together to support our dear friend, Rob Burrow, tragically struck down by Motor Neurone Disease at the age of just 37. JP was there, Kev, Danny Mags, Barrie Mac, Kylie Leuluai, Keith Senior and dozens of others at a bar in Leeds, as well as the old staff, doctors, kitmen and masseurs.

A group of lads brought together by their love of rugby league but bonded through the hours of training and playing, sharing the highs and lows, the blood, sweat and tears. Some of the faces were more familiar. A few have worn better over the years and others, like me I'm sure, have struggled to cope with life since hanging up their boots. But the friendships transcend all of that. The memories and banter we will always share were epitomised by that coming together on such an emotion-charged afternoon to support our mate.

I have made some big decisions in my life and, for the most part, they have come off. Perhaps, because of my upbringing, I am the sort of man who would work hard to make the best of any situation anyway, but I have also enjoyed the most incredible good fortune and met some unbelievable people. I am immensely grateful to every single one of them, more than they will ever know.

On a greying Thursday morning in late July 2023, Tony Smith said he wanted a quiet word, which seemed odd. The previous evening, Halifax had announced that Simon Grix would be standing down at the end of the year and it was heavily rumoured he'd be joining Hull as an assistant in 2024. I thought nothing of it although my dad messaged me to see if I knew anything. Tony told me that he was looking to step back a little bit from hands-on coaching and needed someone with more experience in doing that to plan and deliver the sessions. Simon would fulfil that role and I would no longer be needed. It came as a huge shock, not something I had been expecting. It pulled the rug from under my feet.

I was in the best place I'd been in since I retired from playing. I felt like I was learning, even though I still didn't have any ambitions to be a head coach. I knew I probably wasn't going to be an assistant forever, but hadn't anticipated being put in a position where I had to evaluate where my life was going, within the sport or out of it, for the first time in twenty-five years. I guess I've got another important decision to make about my future as I once again head into the unknown, unsure of which path to go down.

I'm not sure I had the same passion for coaching as I did playing. Maybe I thought it would fill the gap left, but it didn't, it never could. I love some of the conversations and advice I can pass on from my own experiences with players, and I believe I know what it takes to become the best version of yourself, both mentally and physically. I hope I can use that in the future, whether that's with rugby players or transferring it to other walks of life

I understood Tony's decision and where he is in his own coaching career. I totally got that, just didn't see it coming, especially with two years of my deal still to run. That was the biggest surprise.

With fresh uncertainty comes an element of fear about what the next phase of my life will turn out to be. It also feels daunting. People close to me have said I will be alright but, right now, I don't know what that looks like. I have, however, always been of the opinion that things happen for a reason.

One thing is for sure. I won't be taking a backward step.

Gareth Ellis
Career Stats

HEIGHT: 6'2"
WEIGHT: 16.12
POSITION: Second-row.
ALSO PLAYED: Loose-forward, prop, centre, stand-off, wing.

REPRESENTATIVE HONOURS:
18 apps (3t) for Great Britain, 2003-2007
23 apps (4t) for England, 2008-2013
4 apps (1t) for England A, 2002
1 cap (1t) for Yorkshire, 2003

DREAM TEAM: 2003 (centre with Wakefield); 2006, 2007, 2008
(second-row with Leeds); 2016 (second-row with Hull)
WORLD XIII – 2007, 2009, 2011
INTERNATIONAL BACK-ROWER OF THE YEAR – 2008, 2009, 2010

SUPER LEAGUE RECORD:

	APP	T	G	DG	PTS
Wakefield	112 (92+20)	25	2	-	104
Leeds	123 (122+1)	27	1	-	110
Hull	127 (109+18)	21	-	-	84

GREAT BRITAIN

	APP	T	G	DG	PTS
	18 (15+3)	3	-	-	12

ENGLAND

	APP	T	G	DG	PTS
	23 (23+0)	4	-	-	16

ENGLAND A

	APP	T	G	DG	PTS
	4 (4+0)	1	-	-	4

YORKSHIRE

	APP	T	G	DG	PTS
	1 (1+0)	1	-	-	4

TOTALS	408 (366+42)	82	3	-	334

NRL RECORD 2009-2012:

	APP	T	G	DG	PTS
Wests Tigers	75	10	-	-	40

DEBUT: WAKEFIELD v Wigan (sub), Belle Vue. L: 24-60. 12/9/1999.
LEEDS DEBUT: v Canterbury Bulldogs (no 13, WCC), Elland Road.
W: 39-22. 4/3/2005.
WESTS TIGERS DEBUT: v Canberra (no 11), Campbelltown.
W: 34-26. 16/3/2009.
HULL DEBUT: v London (no 11), KCOM Stadium. W: 48-12. 3/5/2013.
TRY HAT-TRICKS: None.
TRY 'DOUBLES': 11 occasions.
WAKEFIELD: 4- (v Wigan, 2002; v Leeds, 2002; v Chorley (Cup), 2004;
v Castleford (a), 2004). LEEDS: 3- (v Widnes, 2005; v Wakefield, 2006;
v Hull, 2008). WESTS TIGERS: 2- (v Penrith, 2010; v Penrith (a), 2011).
HULL: 1- (v Bradford (a), 2014). ENGLAND: 1- (v France, 2010)

CHALLENGE CUP:	36 games (9 tries)
SUPER LEAGUE:	299 games (59 tries, 2 goals)
PLAY-OFFS:	14 games (3 tries)
SUPER-8s:	11 games (2 tries)
WORLD CLUB CHALLENGE:	2 games
NRL:	70 games (9 tries)
NRL PLAY-OFFS:	5 games (1 try)

NOTES

* Amassed 483 career games at club and representative level, scoring 92 tries.
* Played his last game exactly 21 years after debut – for Hull on 13 September 2020 in a 29-16 Challenge Cup win over Castleford (at St Helens)
* Named in Wests Tigers Greatest XIII, a combination from 15 seasons of the merged Wests-Balmain club at the time.
* Made Hull debut on his 32nd birthday in a 48-12 win v London in 2013.
* Played 13 SL play-off games, two for Wakefield in 2004, nine for Leeds between 2005-2008 and three for Hull, the last in their 2017 semi-final loss at Leeds.
* Appeared in five play-off games in NRL for Wests Tigers – including the Tigers' last 'finals-series' appearance, their 20-22 defeat v NZ Warriors in 2011.
* Toured Australasia with GB in 2006, and England for the 2008 World Cup and 2010 Tri-Nations series.

INTERNATIONAL CAREER for ENGLAND:

23 (23+0) appearances, 4 tries

2008 – France (second-row). Toulouse. Won 56-8.
2008 – PNG (World Cup). (second-row). Townsville. Won 32-22.
2008 – Australia (World Cup). (second-row). Melbourne. Lost 4-52.
2008 – New Zealand (World Cup). (second-row). Newcastle. Lost 24-36.
2008 – New Zealand (World Cup SF). (second-row). Brisbane. Lost 22-32.

INTERNATIONAL CAREER for ENGLAND (*continued*):
2009 – Wales (second-row). Bridgend. Won 48-12.
2009 – France (second-row). Doncaster. Won 34-12.
2009 – Australia (second-row). Wigan. Lost 16-26. TRY
2009 – New Zealand (second-row). Huddersfield. Won 20-12.
2009 – Australia (second-row). Final. Elland Road. Lost 16-46.
2010 – France (second-row). Leigh. Won 60-6. TWO TRIES
2010 – NZ Maori (second-row). Auckland. Drew 18-18.
2010 – New Zealand (second-row). Wellington. lost 10-24.
2010 – Australia (second-row). Melbourne. Lost 14-34
2010 – PNG (second-row), Auckland. Won 36-10.
2011 – France (second-row). Avignon. Won 32-18.
2011 – Wales (second-row). Leigh. Won 42-4.
2011 – Australia (second-row). Wembley. Lost 20-36.
2011 – Australia (Final, loose-forward). Elland Rd. lost 8-30.
2012 – Wales (second-row). Wrexham. Won 80-12. TRY
2012 – France (second-row). Hull KR. Won 44-6.
2012 – France (second-row, Final). Salford. Won 48-4.
2013 – Exiles (second-row). Warrington. Won 30-10.

INTERNATIONAL CAREER for GREAT BRITAIN:
18 (15+3) apps, 3 tries
2003 – New Zealand A (second-row). Leeds. Won 52-18. TRY
2003 – Australia (sub). Huddersfield. Lost 12-18.
2004 – Australia (loose-forward). Manchester. Lost 8-12.
2004 – New Zealand (sub). Huddersfield. Won 22-12.
2004 – Australia (sub). Wigan. Won 24-12.
2004 – New Zealand (second-row). Hull. Won 26-24.
2005 – New Zealand (loose-forward). QPR, London. Lost 26-42.
2005 – New Zealand (loose-forward). Huddersfield. Won 38-12.
2005 – Australia (loose-forward). Hull. Lost 14-26.
2006 – New Zealand (second-row). St Helens. Won 46-14.
2006 – New Zealand (second-row). Christchurch. Lost 14-18. TRY

INTERNATIONAL CAREER for GREAT BRITAIN (*continued*):

2006 – Australia (second-row). Sydney. Won 23-12.

2006 – New Zealand (second-row). Wellington. Lost 4-34. TRY

2006 – Australia (second-row). Brisbane. Lost 10-33.

2007 – France (second-row). Leeds. Won 42-14.

2007 – New Zealand (second-row). Huddersfield. Won 20-14.

2007 – New Zealand (second-row). Hull. Won 44-0.

2007 – New Zealand (second-row). Wigan. Won 28-22.

INTERNATIONAL CAREER for ENGLAND A:

4 appearances, 1 try

2002 – NZ A (centre). Brentford. Lost 12-34.

2002 – Fiji (centre). Lautoka. Won 44-8.

2002 – Fiji (centre). Suva. Lost 12-18.

2002 – Tonga (centre). Nuku'alofa. Won 30-18. TRY

MAJOR FINALS

Played 9, Won 6

2005 World Club Challenge – Leeds v Canterbury – Won 39-32

2005 Challenge Cup Final – Leeds v Hull – Lost 24-25

2005 SL Grand Final – Leeds v Bradford – Lost 6-15

2007 SL Grand Final – Leeds v St Helens – Won 33-6

2008 SL Grand Final – Leeds v St Helens – Won 24-16

2008 World Club Challenge – Leeds v Melbourne – Won 11-4

2013 Challenge Cup Final – Hull v Wigan (Captain) – Lost 0-16

2016 Challenge Cup Final – Hull v Warrington (Captain) – Won 12-10

2017 Challenge Cup Final – Hull v Wigan (Captain) – Won 18-14

Investigate our other titles and
stay up to date with all our latest releases at
www.scratchingshedpublishing.co.uk